Library 2

1964

Teach Yourself to Pray

STEPHEN F. WINWARD

Teach
Yourself
to Pray

HARPER & BROTHERS PUBLISHERS
NEW YORK

BV
215
.W54
1961

CONTENTS

Part One

HOW TO PRAY

CONTENTS

CONTENTS

Part Two

MORNING AND EVENING PRAYERS FOR
ONE MONTH

PREFACE

"PRAYER is the Christian's vital breath, the Christian's native air." This truth is widely acknowledged by those "who profess and call themselves Christians", as a result of the efforts of our preachers and teachers, who frequently exhort us to pray. There are also excellent books on the subject of prayer, to many of which the author is deeply indebted. But to teach the vital importance of prayer, and to exhort and urge men to pray, is insufficient. There is too much general exhortation and far too little practical instruction. More attention should be given to method. How can the average busy person converse with God, and live in unbroken fellowship with Him in this twentieth century? Although this book contains a good deal of teaching and a little exhortation, it is not a theoretical treatise about prayer. It is concerned throughout with the practice of prayer. The keyword is HOW.

Following the two general introductory chapters "Why Pray?" and "How to Learn", the rest of the book can be divided into four main parts. Chapters III to VI are entirely concerned with those special periods of personal prayer, the daily morning and evening Quiet Times, which are the basis of the devotional life. The chief kinds of prayer—Adoration, Thanksgiving, Penitence, Petition, Intercession—are then described in Chapters VII to X, with special reference to those Quiet Times. The third main division, Chapters XI to XIII, could be given the title "Total Prayer". Here the keyword is WHOLE—how to pray with the whole personality and with the whole Church. In the last part of the book, Chapters XIV to XVI, we leave behind prayer-times, whether private or public, and consider how to express our devotion to God in our conduct, work, and life in the world.

My indebtedness to other writers is acknowledged in the footnotes. The Scripture quotations are from the REVISED STANDARD VERSION of the Bible, copyrighted 1946 and 1952 by the Division of Christian Education, National Council of Churches, U.S.A., and used by permission.

STEPHEN F. WINWARD

PART ONE

HOW TO PRAY

CHAPTER ONE

WHY PRAY?

WHY teach yourself to pray? Why study a book about it, or give up some time each day to the practice of prayer? It is easy to see why a man should want to teach himself carpentry. He intends perhaps to become a carpenter by occupation, and to earn his living in that way. He may take it up as a hobby, an enjoyable recreation. Or there may be a combination of motives—he will enjoy the work, augment his income, make furniture for the home, have gifts for his friends. But why bother to learn how to pray? Is it really necessary? Apparently not, for many people today seem to get on quite well without it. Is it then a kind of hobby, like gardening or bee-keeping, an optional extra to the main business of living, for which some people have an inclination or aptitude? We shall often be tempted to believe that prayer is no use, and it is certainly not always enjoyable. Why then should we pray? It is necessary to be clear about this at the outset, for if we are to accept the discipline of prayer, we must have adequate incentives. We are likely to persevere only if we believe the quest is really worthwhile. In this chapter we shall state the four main reasons for the practice of prayer.

PRAYER IS FELLOWSHIP WITH GOD

Man has been created for God, and only in fellowship with God can he find fulness of life. We do not know what life is; but we do know that it exists only in relationship. A stone is dead, a horse is alive—a stone cannot enter into relationship with its environment, a horse can. A man can enter into relationship not only with nature, but also with other people in the life of society. If all his personal relationships could be severed, he would be destroyed as a personal being. The richness of our personal life depends upon the quality and depth of our personal relationships. Now the highest relationship possible to man is fellowship with God, apart from

11

which his relationship with nature and with people can never be right and harmonious, satisfying and complete. This relationship is life—a new or higher quality of life; it is eternal life.

In human life we enter into relationship with other persons through meeting and conversation. It is true, of course, nowadays, that communication between persons often takes place at a distance either through the written word, or through the word spoken over the telephone, radio, or television. But usually we get to know people and enter into fellowship with them through direct encounter and conversation. This is also true of the highest relationship possible to man. It is by meeting and conversing with God—that is, by prayer—that we enter into relationship with God, and come to know Him ever more deeply. This does not mean that we can have no knowledge of God at all apart from prayer. Even the prayerless man has to be related in some way to "Him with whom we have to do". Our relationship to nature and especially to people is always, if indirectly, an attitude toward God, even if it be an attitude of indifference or rejection. But a direct personal relationship with God depends upon meeting and conversation. A man who never prays may know a lot about God—only the man who prays can know God. This is the strongest incentive to prayer, and its greatest reward.

The analogy of human friendship is helpful here. Why do we converse with our friends? Not because they are useful to us or confer benefits upon us—although these are frequently among the by-products of friendship. The true reward of friendship is the friend himself. We appreciate his personality, enjoy his company and conversation, find enrichment and fulfilment in the fellowship of giving and receiving. Read the following words of the Psalmist, and it is at once apparent that what he gets out of communion with God is, quite simply, GOD.

"Whom have I in heaven but Thee? And there is nothing on earth that I desire besides Thee. My flesh and my heart may fail, but God is the strength of my heart and my portion for ever" (Psalm 73: 25, 26).

We pray, then, in order to enter into, maintain, and deepen our fellowship with God, whom to know is life eternal.

PRAYER IS GIVING TO GOD

Now this dialogue, this conversation with God which is prayer, has two main aspects; it is a fellowship of giving and receiving. Just as in a mature human relationship there is give and take, so in the activity of prayer we give to and receive from God. In the nature of the case, we receive, or should receive, from God far more than we can ever give to Him. Yet all the same there can be no mature relationship with God apart from both giving and receiving. The giving aspect of prayer is best expressed in the word "offering". In the Bible, worship is essentially something offered to God to the accompaniment of praise and thanksgiving, penitence and petition. We pray in order to give something to God our Creator and Redeemer. "Ascribe to the Lord glory and strength! Ascribe to the Lord the glory due His name; bring an offering and come into His courts" (Psalm 96: 7, 8). We are to offer *praise*, to adore Him, to acknowledge His worth, to appreciate and enjoy what He is in Himself. We are to offer the sacrifice of *thanksgiving*, acknowledging with gratitude all the gifts of God in creation, providence, and redemption. We are to offer *penitence*, the sacrifice of a broken and contrite heart, the humble confession of our imperfection, failure, and sinfulness. We are to offer *ourselves*, to present our bodies as a living sacrifice, holy and acceptable to God. Man was made for God, and by giving to Him ourselves in Adoration and Thanksgiving, in Penitence and Obedience, we fulfil the purpose and the chief end of our being. We pray in order to do this—to offer, to give, to ascribe to the Lord the glory due His name.

PRAYER IS RECEIVING FROM GOD

When King David was offering gifts to God for the building of the Temple, he said, "All things come from Thee, and of Thy own have we given Thee" (I Chronicles 29: 14). We can give to God only those things which we have already received from Him. Prayer cannot be an offering, unless it is first a receiving. We come to God like a woman to the well, with an empty vessel to be filled from the fount of all wisdom, power, and love. Now that which God wills to give us is Himself, and on the human side prayer is opening the door to the Lord who stands and knocks, so that He may come in to have fellowship with us. It is necessary to stress this truth that in prayer we are to receive the Lord Himself, and not just His gifts.

> "If Thou deniest me Thyself, whate'er Thou givest me,
> Empty and void, I languish still, and grieve unceasingly".

If we seek God in prayer only when we want *something*, we are like a boy who goes to his father only when he wants half a crown. We are to go to God to receive Him anew into our lives. This reception takes place in many ways—by waiting on Him in silence, by reading or hearing His word, through meditation and sacrament, and above all in those prayers in which we ask that we may receive. Now if our primary concern is to receive God Himself, then we shall rightly and unselfishly receive also His gifts. Our petitions for these may take the form of "make me" or of "give me". The former type of petition is that God's grace may create or strengthen within us those graces and virtues, those qualities of character and abilities, which will enable us to live the good life. But it is God's will that all our needs—not only our character needs—should be supplied, material as well as spiritual. By making us that which we should be and giving us that which we need, God, through prayer, supplies us with adequate resources for life. This adequacy, this sufficiency, this supply of needed power and resource for living, is one of the rewards of faithful prayer. Even during our prayers of giving we are receiving, for as we offer ourselves to God, we open our lives to Him, and provide the opportunity for which He is always waiting, to give Himself and His gifts to us. Thus prayer is the fellowship of giving and receiving.

PRAYER IS CO-OPERATION WITH GOD

There is a saying of S. Augustine which gives concise expression to one of the fundamental reasons for prayer. "Without God we cannot: without us God will not." God wills to work in partnership with man, and He has so ordered the world that this co-operation is essential. God works among men, not apart from men, but through men. There are many things we cannot do without God; there are many things God will not do without us. The farmer cannot create a harvest, however hard he works; but God does not give him a harvest unless he works. Now this co-operation with God is to take place not only through work, but also through prayer. Indeed it is no exaggeration to say that prayer is the most important way in which man can co-operate with God. As already stated, it is through prayer that we enter into fellowship with God, give ourselves to Him, and receive Him into our lives. It is the supreme way of knowing God's will, and of bringing our wills into harmony with His will. For the object of prayer is not to persuade God to do what I will, but to enable me to know, desire, and do God's will. Like Christ in Gethsemane, we are to pray in order that God's will may be done. Done not only by me—but by all men. Prayer is co-operation with God's purpose in and through the lives of others; it is intercession for the whole creation. It is man working together with God for the achievement of His age-long purpose:

> "*Thy* kingdom come, Thy will be done,
> on earth, as it is in heaven."

SUMMARY

WHY PRAY?

I. Pray in order that you may live in fellowship with God.

II. Pray in order that you may give to God that which is His due—your offerings of praise, thanksgiving, penitence, and an obedient life.

III. Pray in order that you may receive God and His gifts into your life.

IV. Pray in order that you may co-operate with God in achieving His purpose for all mankind.

CHAPTER TWO

HOW TO LEARN TO PRAY

Is it really necessary to learn how to pray? After all, it may be objected, prayer is a native tendency, a natural activity of man. As such it is spontaneous and unlearned. We do not have to learn how to breathe; we begin to do it almost immediately after birth. It is an innate activity, prior to all thought, learning, and experience. Furthermore, it is obvious that the men of God in past ages did not study prayer as a subject, in order to learn how to do it. We cannot imagine Abraham sitting in his tent or Moses tending the sheep, being concerned with the method and technique of prayer! They just prayed—and yet they obviously knew how to pray. William James has said "Many reasons have been given why we should not pray, whilst others are given why we should. But in all this very little is said of the reason why we do pray. The reason why we pray is simply that we cannot help praying". Do we then need to learn how to do something which is spontaneous, inevitable, and natural to man?

NATURAL ACTIVITY AND LEARNING

It is, of course, an error to assume that because an activity is natural (a question-begging word), it does not therefore have to be learned, or cannot be improved by further learning. It is natural for a human being to walk, but we are not born with the ability to do so. We learn to walk, usually with the aid of another, and only after much practice and many a fall. The analogy of speech is even more illuminating, since prayer itself is conversation with God. Speech is natural to man, and yet we all have to learn how to speak. And, unlike walking, in which most normal people reach about the same level of proficiency, people differ enormously in the extent to which they master language and conversation—from the person who can hardly put two words together, to the gifted conversationalist or orator. Prayer is natural to unfallen man, and to fallen man in cer-

16

tain circumstances; yet like speech between men, it must be learned. Certainly Abraham and Moses did not learn how to pray from a book—there are other ways of learning—but they had to learn. If we refuse to take the trouble to learn how to pray, then, if we continue to pray at all, our praying will be immature and childish—which is not the same as childlike. It is by no means rare for men of high intelligence and wide experience to continue to pray in adult life just as they were taught in childhood at their mother's knee. Such men would be unable to say of their prayers "When I was a child, I spoke like a child, I thought like a child, I reasoned like a child; when I became a man I gave up childish ways". (I Corinthians 13: 11). To become a full-grown man in this sphere, it is necessary to give thought and time to the study and practice of prayer. How then can we learn to pray? There are five main ways.

LEARNING BY DOING

In most realms of life, we learn by doing; this is the most important way of learning. It is not possible to learn how to swim by studying a text-book about swimming. The learner must get into the water and make the attempt. This is not to say that the study of theory or technique is of no value. It is frequently helpful and sometimes essential; but it is rarely, if ever, sufficient in itself. The medical student must study his text-books, but he could never become a proficient doctor in that way alone. Some skills are acquired almost entirely by practice— typing, playing tennis, driving a car. This is undoubtedly the most important way of learning how to pray; it is learned in the school of life by practice. It is by praying habitually that we best learn how to pray. The skill of the professional footballer seems to the unthinking onlooker to be "natural" and artless; but in fact it "comes naturally" only as a result of long and arduous practice. Paderewski, the famous Polish pianist, once said "If I stop practising the piano for a day, I notice the difference; if I stop for two days, my family notices the difference; if I stop for three days my friends notice the difference; and if I stop for a week the public notices the difference". In prayer, as in all cases of learning by doing, we shall make many mistakes, get "fed up", and fail again and again. But these mistakes and failures, as in learning to ride a bicycle or to speak

French, can be a valuable part of the process of learning. Resolve then to put into daily practice all that you know about prayer, and all that you read in this book which applies to your own life and situation. *Solvitur ambulando*—just as some of the problems of life are solved not by thinking them out, but by living them out, so the art of prayer is learned, and its difficulties overcome, by praying.

LEARNING BY DOING IT WITH OTHERS

Some things we may learn by doing them alone—but a man could hardly become good at football by playing alone. He must practise, but with others; he learns by playing in a team. We did not learn to speak our native tongue in isolation. As babies and infants we grew up in a family in which the English language was spoken by our parents. We listened to and imitated their words, and learned how to talk by doing it with them. We learn how to talk to God in the same way. It may be that we first learned to pray with our parents at the bedside or in family prayers, and then we learned to pray with that larger family of God, the Church. In the prayer group or meeting, and in corporate worship, through psalms and hymns, through liturgical and free prayer, we learn to pray not only by using the prepared language of others, but by doing it with others. Private and public, personal and corporate prayer, belong together. From the accumulated experience of the Christian community, embodied in the liturgy, the individual may derive unfailing stimulus, enrichment, and help. The importance of this will be fully developed in Chapter XII (PRAYING WITH THE CHURCH).

LEARNING FROM SCRIPTURE AND FROM CHRIST

"The Lord used to speak to Moses face to face, as a man speaks to his friend" (Exodus 33 : 11). Spoken of Moses, these words are also true of many of the great men and women of whom we read in the Bible. They walked with God as intimate friends, listening to His voice and conversing with Him in prayer. We can learn from their experience, and in some cases from their recorded prayers. This is especially true of our Lord Jesus Christ, whose fellowship with the Father was unclouded, perfect, unique. On one occasion, sensing the depth and quality of His prayer life, the disciples came to Him with the request "Lord, teach us to pray" (Luke II: 1). Not only in the pattern prayer, "the Lord's Prayer", which He gave to them in response, but in other sayings and parables, the teaching of Christ on prayer has come down to us. But He not only taught us how to pray—He Himself prayed. When did Jesus pray, how did He pray, what was the content of His prayers? From His example, as well as from His teaching, the disciple may receive both knowledge and inspiration for the prayer life.

> "O Thou by whom we come to God, the life, the truth, the way,
> The path of prayer Thyself hast trod, Lord, teach us how to pray."

LEARNING FROM BOOKS

Saved, taught, and inspired by Christ, many devout men and women in subsequent ages, following in His steps, have trodden that same pathway of prayer. The prayer knowledge and experience of some of them has come down to us in writing. This precious legacy of autobiography and biography, of prayers and devotional classics, of letters and books about prayer, can greatly inform and enrich our devotional thought and practice. A wise learner does not start off from nothing, ignoring all that has hitherto been written on his subject. He makes good use of the books written by others, attempting to assimilate all possible knowledge on the subject, as the basis of original research and experiment. So with prayer. Those who have trodden the way of prayer before us have much to teach us. Some of this teaching and experience is enshrined in books about prayer; some of it in books of prayers. By making use, on occasion, of the prayer-books of others, we can enlarge and enrich our own prayer life. This subject will be dealt with more fully in Chapter XIII (PRAYING FROM BOOKS).

LEARNING FROM THE HOLY SPIRIT

One of the reasons why God gives to us the Holy Spirit to dwell within our hearts is that He may teach us how to pray.

Recognising that we do not know how to pray as we ought, the Lord comes to our aid, and teaches us from within. "Likewise the Spirit helps us in our weakness; for we do not know how to pray as we ought, but the Spirit Himself intercedes for us with sighs too deep for words" (Romans 8: 26). Christ taught His disciples how to pray; the Holy Spirit, continuing His mission in the world, teaches us how to pray. Of course, the Spirit does not work in a vacuum; as already indicated, He teaches us through Scripture, and through the worship and devotional heritage of the Church. But He also operates from within the heart of the believer, inspiring good thoughts and holy desires, giving to us both the impulse and the content of prayer. That is why free or extempore prayer is of such great importance. We must not "quench the Spirit", but leave ample room for His inspired spontaneity, praying as taught by God, who is at work deep within, both to will and to work for His good pleasure.

SUMMARY

There are five main ways in which you can teach yourself to pray:

I. You learn to pray by praying, by acting upon what you already know, by habitual practice.

II. You learn to pray by praying with others in the worshipping community.

III. You learn to pray from the text-book, the Bible, especially from the teaching and example of Jesus Christ.

IV. You learn to pray by reading and studying the devotional writings of others, and by making a judicious use of prayer-books.

V. You learn to pray by being alert and responsive to the inspiration of the Holy Spirit within your heart.

CHAPTER THREE

THE TIME AND PLACE OF PRAYER

ARE PRAYER-TIMES NECESSARY?

IN Chapter I, prayer was described as fellowship with God, in which we give to Him that which is His due, receive Him and His gifts into our lives, and co-operate with Him for the fulfilment of His purposes in the world. But is it not possible to do all this without having fixed or definite times of prayer? Is not the Christian ideal expressed in the familiar words, "It is very meet, right, and our bounden duty, that we should at *all* times, and in *all* places, give thanks unto Thee, O Lord, holy Father, almighty, everlasting God?" The whole of life should be a walk with God, and all times and all places should be sacred to Him. Is it not therefore better to have no fixed or special time or times of prayer, but to pray as often as possible on impulse, or when the need arises, or the circumstances are especially fitting?

There is certainly no justification for *confining* prayer to any special times during the day or the week. There is a sense in which we can and should obey the apostolic precept "Pray without ceasing". Brother Lawrence, whose continual care was to be always with God, could even say, "The time of business does not with me differ from the time of prayer; and in the noise and clatter of my kitchen, while several persons are at the same time calling for different things, I possess God in as great tranquillity as if I were upon my knees at the blessed sacrament." By "the practice of the presence of God", all life can become communion with God, and by doing all things for Him, our daily work can be part of worship. The true objective of the devotional life is finely expressed in the words:

Fill Thou my life, O Lord my God, in every part with praise,
That my whole being may proclaim Thy being and Thy ways.
Not for the lip of praise alone, nor e'en the praising heart
I ask, but for a life made up of praise in every part.

In Chapters XIV, XV, and XVI, we shall be concerned with this basic aim of true devotion, and work out some of its implications. For the present, let us accept it as self-evident that "no part of day or night" should "from sacredness be free: but all my life in every step be fellowship with Thee". The question is, how is it possible to reach, or at least move towards such an objective? How can the ideal be made a reality in our lives?

AN IMPORTANT PRINCIPLE

Here we come upon an important principle: it is by the consecration of one special part, that it becomes possible to consecrate the whole. If all the days of the week are to be holy, then one day of the week, the Lord's Day, must be set aside, be holy to the Lord in a special way. But suppose I do not observe Sunday on the ground that all days are equally sacred, then what happens? Do those who fail to observe the Lord's Day live dedicated lives on Wednesdays and Saturdays? So also, if the whole of a day is to be holy, then it is necessary to set aside, to dedicate, some part of it in a special way to God. Brother Lawrence was able to say "The time of business does not with me differ from the time of prayer", because he observed the time of prayer. It was "when the appointed times of prayer were past" that "he found no difference, because he still continued with God". He did not reach the true objective of devotion by scrapping the appointed times of prayer, but by the observance of them.

THE EXAMPLE OF CHRIST

As stated in Chapter II, one of the ways in which we learn how to pray is by following the example of our Lord Jesus Christ. Now the whole of His life was one great act of prayer—intimate fellowship, perfect offering, complete co-operation. He alone lived the perfect life which was praise in every part. But even He did not realise this objective apart from the formation of definite habits, the observance of special times of prayer. The gospels are not biographies; we have only a selection of the deeds of Jesus. Yet even though our sources of information are scanty, there are suggestive hints and indications. Scholars have suggested that in Mark Chapter I, verses 21 to 39, the evangelist is describing a *typical* day in the life of Jesus. It includes the statement in verse 35, "And in the morning, a great while before day, He rose and went out to a lonely place, and there He prayed". On another occasion, after the Feeding of the Five Thousand, Jesus withdrew for prayer in the evening. "And after He had dismissed the crowds, He went up into the hills by Himself to pray. When evening came, He was there alone" (Matthew 14: 23). We know why Jesus withdrew into the Garden of Gethsemane "on the night when He was betrayed". It was to pray. But only on that occasion? "Now Judas, who betrayed Him, also knew the place; for Jesus *often* met there with His disciples" (John 18: 2). And He who prayed in the mornings and the evenings, had also established the weekly habit of public prayer. "He went to the synagogue as His *custom* was, on the Sabbath day" (Luke 4: 16). If definite times of prayer were necessary even for the Son of God, is it likely that any of us will succeed in living the Christian life without them?

HAVING TIME MEANS MAKING TIME

The character of life in this twentieth century makes it all the more necessary that we should follow the Lord's example of habitual prayer. For most of us, life is full, busy, hectic. There are not enough hours in the day, not enough days in the week, to pack in all that we have to do—or suppose that we have to do. Life can easily degenerate into a hectic round of duties and pleasures, a frantic rushing hither and thither. If we leave prayer to fit into the appropriate time—well, it just doesn't fit, there is no appropriate time. It is simply crowded out. We become like Martha of Bethany, preoccupied with preparing an elaborate meal, when one course would have been sufficient. "Distracted with much serving" and "anxious and troubled about many things", she had no time to sit at the feet of Jesus and listen to His words (Luke 10: 38–42). If we are to have time, we must make time—that is—deliberately set it aside. A result may be that some other things are crowded out. Would that necessarily matter? In any case it would be preferable to crowding God out, since we have been created for Him.

HAVING A RULE OF PRAYER

It is helpful to have a rule of prayer: to set aside certain definite times each day for keeping tryst with the Lord. Daniel "got down upon his knees three times a day and prayed and gave thanks before his God" (Daniel 6: 10). The Christian apostles also observed the set hours of prayer (See The Acts 3: 1, and 10: 9). Such a rule should be a help and guide, not a master or tyrant. It should not be rigid and inflexible. There are circumstances when it is legitimate and sensible to set aside such a rule—it may be because of sickness or because of urgent duty or need. It may be wrong if it interferes with our obligations to others—on the other hand, it will certainly be wrong if it does *not* interfere with our own laziness and indiscipline. We must not be soft with ourselves, and a rule can help us in the struggle against slackness, sloth, and indiscipline. We should regard these fixed times as appointments with the Lord, to be kept. Now it is not possible, or rather it is not wise, to generalise about such a rule of prayer. Because the character and temperament, the needs and circumstances, of each individual are unique, each one of us must make his own rule. But there is one important principle we should all bear in mind in making it. It is a self-evident truth, it is obviously fitting, that we should begin and end each day with the Lord. We may be able to have other Quiet Times during the day, but—unless unavoidably prevented—we should all aim at starting and finishing each day in communion with God. Thus each separate day is set in the framework of prayer, with a view to consecrating all that lies between. "From the rising of the sun to its setting, the name of the Lord is to be praised" (Psalm 113: 3).

MORNING PRAYER

So very much of what we read, hear, and learn about prayer is made null and void by our failure to get up at the right time in the morning. For it is only by rising in time that there can be adequate time for prayer at the beginning of the day. At least, this is true of all who have to start work at a definite hour. If I don't get up in time, I shall not have time for prayer; and if I haven't time for prayer, I shall not pray—it's as simple as that. A good alarum clock is a useful piece of equipment for the devotional life! What amount of time should be given to morning prayer? This is a matter upon which it is unwise to generalise. Some find that one hour is not too much; others are satisfied with half an hour, or twenty minutes. Those who find this an exceptionally hard discipline, would be wise to aim at a minimum of ten minutes to begin with, and perhaps to increase it gradually as the habit becomes well established. Whatever the length of time, it should never be hurried; one should not destroy the sense of leisure by trying to pack too much into it. Where should the morning Quiet Time fit into the pattern of the day? The ideal is to rise, wash, and dress first. This helps to ensure (especially if the water is cold!) that one is fully awake, and there is also much to be said for coming to God, not unwashed, unshaven, or in a dressing-gown, but clothed and smart. It is a mistake, although a common one, to suppose that externals do not matter in the spiritual life. This ideal of morning prayer in the bedroom, after dressing, before breakfast, may be difficult for those who share a room, especially if the other or others are unsympathetic. It may be impossible for the mother with a baby to tend, or for the housewife who has to prepare a very early breakfast for her husband or children. Wives and mothers may find that the best time for prayer is immediately after the men have left for work or the children for school. Some have opportunity to read while travelling to work by bus or train, and, although it is not ideal, it is possible to pray while walking or travelling by public transport to work. For it is possible to pray without anyone knowing you are doing it. Others may find time on arriving at the place of work, or by dropping into a church on the way. The best time for you—as close as possible to the beginning of the day—for at least ten minutes, and if you can for twenty or thirty minutes—these suggestions can be of help in making your own rule of prayer.

EVENING PRAYER

It is not so difficult to set aside time at the other end of the day for prayer. Work is done, and there is a sense of leisure, of not having to finish at a certain time. There is much more time available, as much as we require for scripture reading, meditation, and prayer. For many, perhaps most, the best time for evening prayer is on retiring to the bedroom for the night. And there is very great value in thinking of God and speaking to Him last thing at night. Our last thoughts sink down deeply into the mind, and may continue to work within us while we sleep. "For He gives to His beloved in sleep" (Psalm 127: 2). On the other hand, there are others who habitually feel "dead beat" last thing at night. They find it difficult to keep awake and hard to concentrate. For all such there may be something better than to offer to God the "fag-end" of the day. There may be an opportunity earlier, perhaps just after the evening meal, while the mind is still fresh and alert, for quiet reading and prayer. What is best for one may not be for another. In praying, as in giving, "each one must do as he has made up his mind" (II Corinthians 9: 7).

THE PLACE OF PRAYER

There is something to learn both from the teaching and the example of·Christ, about the place of prayer. Jesus did not think that all places were suitable—the street corner, for example! "But when you pray, go into your room and shut the door and pray to your Father who is in secret; and your Father who sees in secret will reward you" (Matthew 6: 6). The picturesque detail about shutting the door, as well as the context, provides the necessary clue for interpreting this explicit instruction about the place of prayer. If possible, we are to be alone *when we are at private prayer*—corporate prayer is another matter. When we offer private prayer in public, there is always the temptation to play-acting, as well as the likelihood of interruption and distraction. It may of course, be impossible to get alone in the house, if "your room" is shared with others. It was rarely possible for Jesus Himself as an itinerant teacher and healer. That no doubt is why we read of Him going out of the house, to pray in a solitary place (Mark 1: 35). As He retired to the lonely spot, the hill-side, the desert, the garden, so we may be able, at least sometimes, to do the same. Those situations in which we cannot ever get alone—on board ship, in the barracks, the school dormitory—are admittedly difficult testing-times. But when we cannot do a thing, desirable in itself, God makes it up to us in some mysterious way. We are given special grace to pray where we must. The bedroom, however, for most folk, most of the time, will be the normal place of prayer. It may be helpful to have a special prayer-corner within it. Leaning against the bed, with its powerful suggestion of sleep, may not be the best place to pray. A strong, small table, in front of which it is possible to kneel, and on which the elbows may be rested, is a help. On the wall behind it, there may be a helpful picture of Christ, or a cross, or a crucifix. On the table keep the Bible, and your own prayer and devotional books. We may conclude with the words of Richard Baxter: "Concerning the fittest place for heavenly meditation, it is sufficient to say that the most convenient is some private retirement. Therefore withdraw thyself from all society, even the society of godly men, that thou mayest awhile enjoy the society of the Lord."

SUMMARY

I. It is necessary to observe special times of prayer each day, for only in this way can the whole of life be fellowship with God.

II. In doing this, we are following the example of Jesus Christ.

III. In the busy modern world, we shall only have time if we make time for prayer.

IV. It is advisable to make a rule of prayer, setting aside some time each morning and each evening for fellowship with God.

V. Each person must decide for himself where the morning and evening Quiet Times best fit into the pattern of the day, and the amount of time to be given to them.

VI. The right place for prayer is the quiet room or the solitary place.

CHAPTER FOUR

BIBLE READING AND MEDITATION

LET us now suppose that we have decided to keep tryst daily with God, to have a Quiet Time in the morning and evening of each day. Another question then arises. How shall we best use the time? What is to be done during that ten or thirty minutes set aside for communion with the Lord? An attempt will be made to answer that question in detail, in this and the two following chapters. There are two main elements in a Quiet Time. The devotional reading of the Bible, and the offering of our prayers. In this chapter we shall be concerned with the former, and in Chapters V and VI with the latter.

THE PURPOSE OF BIBLE READING

Why should the Bible be read during the period set apart for prayer? It is important to get this clear at the outset. Although no hard and fast line can be drawn between them, it will be helpful here to make a distinction between Bible study and the devotional reading of the Bible. We study the Bible to get acquainted with its background, contents, and message. This is a necessary discipline for some, and helpful to all. But this is not the reason why the Bible should be read during a Quiet Time. For then we have an appointment with "the Lord and King of Scripture", we are keeping tryst with Him. We read the Bible devotionally in order to meet with God, and to listen to Him speaking through His word. The primary purpose is not to learn something about or from a book, but to meet with a Person, to encounter the Eternal God who is revealed in His living Word, Jesus Christ our Lord. For He is the Word of God, hidden in the Old Testament, revealed in the New. To borrow an illustration from Martin Luther, Christ in scripture is like a baby in a crib. We go to the crib for the sake of the one who is in it. Otherwise we merit Christ's rebuke to the Bible students of His day: "You search the scriptures, because you think that in them you have eternal life; and it is they that bear witness to Me; yet you refuse to come to Me that you may have life" (John 5: 39, 40). To draw near to the Lord, to meet with Him, to listen to Him through His word—that is why we are to read the Bible during prayer-time.

HOW GOD SPEAKS

When God called Samuel in the temple at Shiloh, he responded "speak, for Thy servant hears" (I Samuel 3: 10). That is the attitude in which to approach the Bible reading, with listening ears and mind alert for what God has to say. But what is meant by saying that God "speaks" through the Bible? Do we hear a voice addressing us in Hebrew, Greek, English, or some other language? Take the analogy of a personal letter, received by post from a close friend. Through the written words of the letter the friend may reveal his mind and purpose, he may convey a message or make a request, he may rebuke or encourage, ask questions or give directions. Someone seeing you reading such a letter might well inquire "What does your friend say?" Say! He speaks through the written word. "The Bible is a letter from God, with my personal address on it." Through the written word, His word, the Lord is active, revealing His nature and purpose, rebuking and challenging, encouraging and comforting, strengthening and directing us. All devout readers of the Bible know from experience what happens, however difficult it may be to find words which adequately express it. You read a passage, and something "strikes" you, "finds" you, "speaks" to your condition. "I felt that it had been written just for me." We are addressed by a Person through the words of a book.

HOW TO READ THE BIBLE

How should the portions to be read during the Quiet Time be selected? The following suggestions may serve as a general guide.

I. It is better to read little rather than much. The length of the passage to be read will depend on the time available. But it is better to ponder deeply on a little than to skim superficially over a lot. One story, one paragraph, one unit of material should suffice. There is no necessary virtue in reading one chapter at a time. The chapter and verse divisions were not inserted until the Middle Ages, and they are not always in the right places. A good Bible reader is not like a swift skimming over the surface of a pond, but like a miner digging for hidden treasure. Read a little, and read it well.

II. Read progressively through one selected book of the Bible. The practice of reading haphazardly has little to commend it. The Bible is not made up of isolated texts and disconnected passages. Each book is a unity and should be read as such. We are to hear the message of the whole as well as of the parts.

III. How should the books of the Bible themselves be selected for reading? Is there any priority? Should the beginner start with Genesis and plod right on to The Revelation? It is better to begin with the New Testament, and by reading the Gospels. A sound knowledge of the life, teaching, death, and resurrection of Christ, is essential to an understanding of the rest of the New Testament; and it is better to read the Old Testament in the light of its fulfilment in the New. There is also much to be said for reading together books of the same type—the Law books, the History books, the Wisdom literature, the Hebrew Prophets, the Epistles of Paul, the Gospel and Epistles of John; or books which belong together like Leviticus and Hebrews, Daniel and The Revelation.

IV. In reading the Bible devotionally, one should not hesitate to skip unsuitable passages. Why read through the nine chapters of names with which the First Book of Chronicles opens? Why read all the detailed regulations for animal sacrifice in the Book of Leviticus, or the many chapters in the Book of Joshua which decribe how the land was divided among the Hebrew tribes? This is not to question the inspiration and authority of the *whole* Bible, for which God has many other uses in addition to the one we are now considering. Do not wade through passages just for the sake of saying that you have read every word. Just as some parts of the Bible are never read in public worship, so some parts are unsuitable for private prayer. Passages obviously unsuitable *for this special purpose* should be omitted.

V. There are certain books or parts of the Bible which the reader will be unable to understand, without the aid of an interpreter. Much of the Bible speaks directly to the wayfaring man; but there are other parts which will be virtually meaningless to him. Unaided, he will be able to make little of, say, the Book of Nahum, the Night Visions of Zechariah, the theology of the Epistle to the Romans, or the symbolism of Daniel and The Revelation. Many people start off and subsequently give up reading the Bible because they just cannot understand it. But why read it, or at least why read these more difficult parts, unaided? Let us go on now to consider the aids which have been provided.

BIBLE-READING NOTES

Guided by the Holy Spirit, the evangelist Philip overtook an Ethiopian eunuch who was reading the Book of Isaiah in his chariot, and put to him the question "Do you understand what you are reading?" The Ethiopian replied "How can I, unless someone guides me?" (The Acts 8: 30, 31). God then spoke to the eunuch through the written word *interpreted* by Philip. There is much that we do not understand in the Bible, but God had provided the interpreters. The book and the fellowship, Bible and Church, belong together, and the Lord has set within the Church preachers and teachers, commentators and writers, scholars and interpreters. We can take these with us into our Quiet Times, by making use of the expositions or notes they have written. Why then read the difficult parts of the Bible without a clue, when the clue has been provided? The best method of Bible reading for most of us may well be the use of some system of daily readings with explanatory notes and devotional aids. The three best known in this country and in English-speaking lands overseas are the International Bible Reading Association,[1] the Bible Reading Fellowship,[2] and the Scripture Union.[3] The Bible Reading Fellowship is Anglican, and the Scripture Union notes are suitable for evangelical Christians of conservative theology. All three systems have notes for different age groups, and for simple or more advanced study. It is true, of course, that as we continue to hear or read the Bible interpreted by others, the less need there

[1] Central Hall Buildings, Durnsford Road, London, S.W.19

[2] 171 Victoria Street, London, S.W.1

[3] 5 Wigmore Street, London W.1

will be of aids of this kind. Insights once gained remain; our
knowledge of the word grows. But for the learner, the best
rule is—have your eyes on the book and your ears open to
Philip.

HOW TO READ THE DAILY PORTION

I. You are reading the Bible in order to draw near to the
Lord and listen to His word; come then with reverence and
expectancy. Such an attitude best finds expression in a brief
prayer for illumination. Ask the Holy Spirit who inspired the
word, to come and interpret it to you. Pray in your own words,
or use the following scriptures:

Speak, Lord, for Thy servant heareth.

Open my eyes, that I may behold wondrous things out of
Thy law.

II. Then read through the selected passage slowly. Skimming
through a reading hurriedly is of very little value. In the Book
of Job it is said of the miner deep down within the earth "his
eye sees every precious thing" (28: 10). Reading the Bible is
like mining; we have to dig deep down to find the hidden
treasure. This takes time, and our reading should therefore
be relaxed and leisurely.

III. Make full use of the intellect to understand the passage
as fully as possible. Ask yourself all kinds of questions about
it. What—when—why—how—who? What is the main point,
the principle truth in this story, incident, or parable? What
does it teach me about God, about other people, about life,
about myself? Do I understand the meaning of all the words
used? Do other passages in the Bible shed any further light
on it? After having thought out the meaning fully for yourself,
then, if you are using a system of notes, read the notes for
additional light on the passage. Do this *after* your own thinking, lest the insights of others become a substitute for your own
thought.

IV. If the portion read is a story, use your imagination to
picture the whole scene. "Open my eyes, that I may behold
wondrous things"—this can be true in a special sense of the
imagination. Visualise the scene, and see "in your mind's eye"
all the characters playing their parts as in a drama. Even when
a reading is not story or incident, its truth can often be "seen".

For example, how many pictures are there in Matthew Chapter VII? The Bible is an art-gallery; its language is concrete, vivid, picturesque. You can *see* as well as hear the word of God.

V. After the intellect and the imagination—the will; after the mind and the eyes, the hands, the practical out-working or application. What is the Lord saying to me through the written word, with reference to my own life and situation? What have I got to be, to do or to say, as a result of this reading? For we hear the word of God in order that we may do it (Matthew 7: 24). In education, the importance of what is called "expression work" is now widely recognised. We retain that which we have heard and seen by doing it. For the Psalmist, God's word is not only for the ears and the eyes. "Thy word is a lamp to my feet and a light to my path" (Psalm 119: 105). Let us live it out.

SUMMARY

I. Why read the Bible at prayer-time? In order to meet with God and listen to His word.

II. How does God speak? The Bible is like a letter from a friend; God uses the written word to communicate personal messages and convictions to the reader.

III. How should the Bible be read? Read a little thoroughly— read through one selected book—read the New Testament before the Old—omit passages unsuitable for devotional reading—use notes for the interpretation of difficult parts.

IV. God has set men within the Church to help us understand the Bible; we accept their help by making use of Bible-reading notes.

V. How should I read the daily portion? Pray for help—read the passage slowly—think deeply about it—picture the scene—apply it to your life.

CHAPTER FIVE

THE CONTENT OF OUR PRAYERS

WHAT SHOULD I PRAY ABOUT?

PRAYER is conversation with God; but conversation itself is a dialogue, not a monologue. It is a two-way traffic street; it involves both listening and speaking. If you go for a walk with a friend, it will not be very satisfactory if he does all the speaking and you do all the listening. Nor will the situation be improved if you do all the speaking and your companion all the listening. Communion involves both listening and speaking —and so it is with God. In the last chapter we were concerned with the listening. Through the devotional reading of the Bible, we listen to God speaking through the written word. We turn now to the other side of communion, to the other main strand in a Quiet Time—speaking to God in prayer. And we shall first of all consider what is to many people the most difficult problem of the prayer life—the *content* of our prayers. The difficulty may be expressed like this. "What should I pray about? My trouble is, when I get on my knees, I just don't know what to say. As a result, I find myself saying the same things over and over again, using well-worn clichés and threadbare sentences, offering the same few petitions, until the whole thing becomes thoroughly stale, dull, and unreal." Much of what is written in this book will have some bearing on this problem, especially what is said in Chapters VII to X on THE CHIEF KINDS OF PRAYER, and in Chapter XIII on PRAYING FROM BOOKS. In this present chapter four ways of giving a more ample and varied content to our prayers will be described.

TAKE YOUR BIBLE READING INTO YOUR PRAYERS

Normally in a Quiet Time, the devotional reading of the Bible should precede, not all prayer, but the main time of prayer. We should listen to God before speaking to God. In normal conversation what I say to the other person bears some relationship to what he has just said to me. If then, God has spoken to me through the reading of His word, my reply to Him in prayer should be in the nature of a response. Prayer is man's response to God's revelation, the human answer to Him who reveals and communicates Himself through the word. This means that what has been read in the Bible will enter into the subsequent prayers. It is likely that the Bible reading as a whole will suggest several subjects for prayer—for thanksgiving and confession, for personal petition and intercession. Suppose, for example, that you have been reading and meditating on the story of Christ stilling the storm on the Sea of Galilee. As a result of the reading you may be led by the Holy Spirit to give thanks for Christ's faith, courage, and serenity; to confess your own cowardice in the face of trial and danger; to ask for yourself the faith of which Christ speaks; and to intercede "for those in peril on the sea" (Mark 4: 35–41). There are few, if any, Bible passages which do not suggest some subject for prayer. In the last section of the previous chapter—"How to read the daily portion"—a certain sequence was suggested; after thought and imagination, application. How am I to *do* the truth, how am I to express this in my life? These insights, directions, resolutions, should be turned into prayers. We ask God for wisdom, guidance, and strength to do that which we have heard in His word. Prayer thus inspired by the Bible has this great merit and advantage. Since God Himself, His nature and purpose, is revealed in the Scriptures, it will be prayer in harmony with His character and will, prayer "in His Name".

TAKE THE COMING DAY INTO YOUR PRAYERS

If the Bible is the Christian's prayer-book, so also is daily life. Content to our prayers will be given not only by the Scriptures, but by the circumstances of the day itself. Each separate day may be likened to the page of a book; as we read that page and meditate on it, the Holy Spirit will reveal to us what to pray about. At the time of morning prayer, it is a good thing to look ahead, to anticipate as far as possible the life of the coming day. Not that the events of each day can be exactly foreseen, for there is always the unknown, the unpredictable element in life. There are the surprises, painful or joyful, the sudden temptations or opportunities, the unexpected demands or events. On the other hand, much of the life of an ordinary day can be foreseen, and we may pray over it in advance. Put to yourself three questions: "*Whom* shall I be meeting today? *Where* shall I be going today? *What* shall I be doing today?" The answers to these three questions will bring to mind people, situations, tasks, about some of which you ought to pray. One of the lessons we may learn from the example of Jesus Christ, is to pray about things in advance. Before He selected the twelve men who were to be the nucleus of the Church, He spent all the previous night in prayer to God (Luke 6: 12). Later on, He prayed before putting to those same Apostles the great question "Who do you say that I am?" (Luke 9: 18). He anticipated the last and greatest day of His life on earth with prayer (Luke 22: 39–46). This last reference is doubly instructive. The Apostles who were bidden to pray in Gethsemane, but failed to do so, were unready when the crisis came. The Master who prayed, was ready for anything, and completely victorious. It can make all the difference to a day, if we pray about it in advance, bringing the people we are likely to meet, the tasks waiting to be done, and the decisions which have to be made, to God in prayer. He who does this, will have plenty of material for prayer.

TAKE THE PAST DAY INTO YOUR PRAYERS

During the evening Quiet Time, the day may be taken up into our prayers in retrospect. We now look back over the day which is past, quietly reviewing its events in the presence of God. Three direct questions will provide material for confession, for intercession, and for thanksgiving. "What wrong have I done this day, or what good have I left undone?" Examine your heart, confess your sins of commission and omission, and ask for forgiveness. "Of the people I have met or heard about today, are any in need of my prayers?" Then pray for each person according to his need. "What joys, gifts, mercies, blessings, have I received this day?" Express your gratitude to God for each one of them. Not only the past, but also the coming day may be taken up into evening prayers. The familiar petition in the Lord's Prayer "Give us this day our daily bread" may also be translated "Give us today bread for the coming day". The biblical day began at sunset. "And there was evening and there was morning, one day" (Genesis 1:5). The evening Quiet Time may indeed be the real beginning of "the coming day", because we prepare for that day by praying over it in advance. Those who keep the daily tryst with God only in the evenings (and they are legion), may well combine the suggestions of this and the previous section, praying first over the past day and then over the coming day. The essential thing is to bring each day to God. The manna in the wilderness, God's own provision for His pilgrim people, had to be gathered every day. It could not be gathered and stored up for future use (Exodus 16:13–21).

'Day by day', the promise reads; daily strength for daily needs.

TAKE YOUR DESIRES INTO YOUR PRAYERS

One of the best definitions of prayer is to be found in the first two lines of a hymn by James Montgomery.

> Prayer is the soul's sincere desire,
> Uttered or unexpressed.

Prayer is desire. The desire may be expressed in words—prayers —or it may be too deep for words. Here we come upon the real distinction between praying and merely saying prayers. Real prayers, whether extempore or liturgical, are the expression in words of the desire or desires of those who are uttering them. Prayer without desire is "vain repetition", a matter of empty words. But God does not listen to polite speeches; He hears those prayers which, however inadequately, articulate the real desires of the heart. Therefore—and this is the point—if our prayers are to have full content, they must express our real desires. It is just because we often fail here that prayer seems unreal. It is insincere because we are not bringing to God our true interests, concerns, and desires. A young man of twenty is keenly interested in engineering, his job, in football, his recreation, and of course in Mary, his fiancée, whom he hopes to marry shortly. But none of these interests is brought into his prayers because, he supposes, they are not "religious". He always prays about churches and ministers, missionaries and the sick, in none of which (unfortunately) he is particularly interested. He wonders why prayer is so dull and unreal, and is tempted to give it up. He must be helped to realise that religious experience is not a special kind of experience, fenced off from life; it is ordinary experience seen in depth, in relationship to God. He must be encouraged to pray about his real interests, to express his deep desires in prayer, whatever they may be. We should always bring our strong desires to God in prayer, even if it be to ask forgiveness for them. All that has been said in this and in the two preceding sections of this chapter may be summed up as follows: bring your life into your prayers—your daily life, tasks, relationships, concerns, interests, and desires. He who brings his life into his prayers will have a full prayer life—unless, of course, his life itself is dull and empty. In that case there is no remedy short of doing something about life as a whole. For we cannot live one way and pray another. The content of our prayers can only be as rich and varied as the content of our life. Great praying presupposes great living. Prayer and life are one.

SUMMARY

What should I pray about? How can I give to my prayers a full and varied content?

I. Pray about your Bible reading. Let the passage as a whole suggest topics for prayers, and pray about the practical directions and resolutions which are the outcome of your meditation upon it.

II. Pray about the coming day—the people you are to meet, the events and situations you can foresee, the tasks you have to do.

III. Pray about the past day—confessing sins, interceding for people in need, giving thanks for blessings.

IV. Pray about your sincere desires and vital interests.

CHAPTER SIX

THE PATTERN OF OUR PRAYERS

PRAYER—PLANNED OR SPONTANEOUS?

SHOULD a Quiet Time be planned? Should there be any order or sequence in the offering of our prayers? Or is it better to forget all about a pattern, and give spontaneous expression in prayer to whatever thoughts and desires enter the mind? We are familiar nowadays with the difference between a planned and an unplanned city. In former times, especially during the Industrial Revolution, many of our towns just grew higgledy-piggledy, an ugly jumble of unplanned streets. In pleasing contrast is the modern town or suburb, with industrial and residential areas, central shops and public buildings, pattern and beauty. Obviously a town should be planned. On the other hand, there are aspects of life which cannot be planned. It is hardly possible and it is certainly not desirable to plan a romance or a friendship; spontaneity is the essence of it. Between these extremes, there are other spheres of life where both planning and spontaneity are of value. A holiday requires a little planning—yet not too much, for without freedom to follow the inclinations of the moment, it would hardly be a holiday. What about prayer? Should it be planned or spontaneous or both? There are those who believe that prayer, public as well as private, should be unplanned. It should be as free as the wind, extempore, a manifestation of the "inspired spontaneity" of the Holy Spirit. To plan prayer is to quench the Spirit. At the other extreme are those for whom private prayer is largely the recitation of orders or offices, and public prayer a fixed liturgy. Rarely do we find these extremes in practice; it is rather a matter of degree and emphasis. It is our conviction that private, like public prayer, is at its best when there is a combination of planning and freedom, of order and spontaneity. There should be a flexible pattern which allows ample room for the free movement of the Spirit: the Spirit of order and of liberty. In this chapter we shall study the principles underlying the formation of such a pattern, and conclude with a number of suggested outlines for the Quiet Time.

THE PATTERN PRAYER

"He was praying in a certain place, and when He ceased, one of His disciples said to Him, 'Lord, teach us to pray, as John taught his disciples'" (Luke 11: 1). In response to this request, the Lord Jesus gave to His disciples the pattern or model prayer. It is found in Luke 11, verses 2 to 4, and also in Matthew 6, verses 9 to 13. The latter version is more familiar to us because of its use in the liturgy. The prayer consists of an address and six petitions—the doxology is not part of the original prayer, but was added later. This is the Lord's Prayer, the perfect pattern He gave for the instruction and guidance of His disciples. What may we learn from it?

I. God Himself should come first, and be the centre of all our prayers. Of the six petitions, the first three have to do with God. Trusting in His love, submitting to His authority, conscious of His greatness, we address Him as "our Father who art in heaven". We pray about His name, asking that we may reverence His character, stand in awe of His revealed nature. We pray about His kingdom, asking that God will come to reign in power and love over all His creatures. We pray about His will, asking that we and all who dwell on earth may obey Him, as He is already obeyed in heaven. Here Jesus Christ is saying "in your prayers, put God first, give Him the supreme place, desire above all His glory". Only when God is put first can we rightly pray for others and present our own personal petitions. This means that Praise and Adoration, Thanksgiving and Oblation, will have priority and prominence in the prayers of the Christian.

II. We should be concerned with the needs of others as well as with our own basic needs. The second part of the pattern prayer is concerned with the needs of man. It consists of three petitions. We pray for daily food, for that nourishment of body and spirit without which we cannot live. We pray for the forgiveness of our sins in proportion as we ourselves forgive those who have sinned against us. We pray that because of the frailty of our nature we may not be exposed to temptation; but since we cannot always avoid it, we ask for God's strength to overcome evil. Here Jesus Christ teaches us to bring our essential needs to God. So often we are concerned with what we want and what is secondary. Our primal needs are food, forgiveness and moral strength. But it is not just for my own basic needs that I am to pray. This is a family or social prayer, addressed not to "my Father" but to "*our* Father". I am taught to pray "give *us* . . . bread, forgive *us* our trespasses, deliver *us* from evil". I am to be concerned about the basic needs of others, as well as my own. Prayer is to be other-centred, as well as God-centred. Intercession—prayer for others—is to be as important as personal petition.

III. In the first part of the Lord's Prayer we are obeying the great commandment: "The Lord our God, the Lord is one; and you shall love the Lord your God with all your heart, and with all your soul, and with all your mind, and with all your strength" (Mark 12: 29, 30). In the second part of the Lord's Prayer, we are obeying the second commandment of Christ: "You shall love your neighbour as yourself" (Mark 12: 31). As yourself—there is a right kind of self-love. He who is as concerned for the needs of others as for his own, will be rightly concerned with his own needs. Here then we have the true pattern, the right order for prayer—God, others, myself. Not as in grammar, I—thou—he; but the reverse, He (God)—thou (neighbour)—I. The pattern of the Quiet Time should reflect this essential order. God first—Adoration, Submission to His will revealed in Scripture, Thanksgiving; neighbour second—Intercession; myself last—personal Petition. Here is a prayer which admirably sums up the teaching of the pattern prayer.

O Lord God, so order our doings that we may observe in all things the perfect rule of Christ, and set ourselves to serve Thee first, others next, and ourselves last; through the same Jesus Christ our Lord.

THE PATTERN OF LISTENING AND SPEAKING

So far it has been stated that our prayers should reflect the structure, the true order of life—God, others, myself. But there is another pattern to be considered. As stated earlier, communion with God is a dialogue, a two-way conversation. There is a rhythm of revelation and response, of Divine Word and human answer, of listening and speaking. Because the Divine word is prior to the human response, the Quiet Time should have the pattern—listening, speaking. This pattern may be illustrated from the original Christian service, the Eucharist or Lord's Supper. This service has two main parts. First comes "the liturgy of the word", the reading of the Old Testament, the Epistle and the Gospel, followed by the teaching or preaching of the word. Here the congregation is listening to the word of God read and expounded. In the second part of the service, there is response to the word in the intercessions, in the offertory of bread, wine, and money, in the great prayer of thanksgiving, which consecrates, and in the oblation of the worshippers as a living sacrifice. The first main part of a Quiet Time should likewise be devoted to listening to the word. As described in Chapter IV, we read the Holy Scriptures and meditate on them, that we may hear and obey the word of God. A Quiet Time is, as the phrase implies, a listening time. After this, we respond to God's word by speaking to Him in prayer. We offer Thanksgiving, Intercession, Petition, and the Oblation of our own lives. It is always helpful to keep this rhythm in mind when planning a Quiet Time. It is a common mistake to rush into the presence of God and start talking—and to keep on talking throughout the whole period of prayer. "You have two ears and one mouth; so listen twice as much as you speak." This is a good rule for life, and an excellent rule for the devotional life. This then is the pattern—listen, listen, speak.

BALANCED PRAYER

There is one other important truth which should be kept in mind in the planning of a Quiet Time. We usally speak about prayer in the singular, but there are several different kinds of prayer. Water is not an element but a compound, made up of hydrogen and oxygen. Prayer, too, is a compound—it is Adoration, Thanksgiving, Penitence, Intercession, Petition. In Chapters VII, VIII, IX and X of this book, a full account will be given of these chief kinds of prayer. Here, we are simply concerned to make the point, that if the prayer life is to be whole, complete, balanced, all these different kinds of prayer must be included in the pattern. It becomes unbalanced if any of the main parts is omitted, or if the part is mistaken for the whole. For example, some, indeed many people assume that prayer is just asking for things for oneself. But when prayer is Petition and nothing else, it almost inevitably becomes self-centred. Others, seeing this, have gone to the other extreme; they have dropped Petition in favour of Adoration, seeking God for His own sake alone. Some are given to excessive Self-examination; they are always probing into their souls and confessing their sins, real and imaginary. They would be better employed praising God and giving thanks to Him for all His goodness. Others are spiritually unhealthy for the opposite reason; they rarely, if ever, examine their hearts and confess their sins. We hear a good deal nowadays about the importance of a balanced diet. That is what is needed in the prayer life. It is not suggested that all the main kinds of prayer should be offered in every Quiet Time; but they should all have some place in the devotional life. It is helpful sometimes to devote a whole Quiet Time to just one of the five main aspects of prayer. For example, it is appropriate at the end of the week to make a full self-examination, followed by confession and a prayer for pardon. Make your own patterns of prayer and vary them from time to time. Here are four examples.

PATTERNS OF PRAYER

Morning Prayer

Prayer for Illumination of the Scriptures
Scripture Reading and Meditation
Prayers arising from Scripture
Prayers for the Coming Day
Act of Surrender

Evening Prayer

Quiet Review of the Past Day
Penitence (confession of any sin or negligence today)
Intercession (for those you have met or those in need)
Thanksgiving (for the joys, gifts, and blessings of today)

Morning Prayer

Adoration (A Psalm or a Hymn)
Thanksgiving
Petitions for Today
The Lord's Prayer

Evening Prayer

Confession of Sin
Scripture Reading and Meditation
Intercession
Commend yourself to God

SUMMARY

I. In private prayer, planning and freedom, order and spontaneity should be combined. Have a flexible plan for the Quiet Time.

II. In the Lord's Prayer, Jesus Christ taught us to put God first, and to be concerned about the needs of others, as well as our own. The pattern is God—neighbour—myself.

III. Communion with God has the two aspects of listening and speaking. In the first part of a Quiet Time, we listen to God through His word; our prayers are a response to this.

IV. There are five main kinds of prayer—Adoration, Thanksgiving, Penitence, Intercession and Petition. They must all be included in the pattern for prayer.

CHAPTER SEVEN

ADORATION AND THANKSGIVING

When a white ray of sunlight is passed through a triangular glass prism, it is broken up into all the colours of the spectrum, from red to violet. Like that single ray of light, prayer can be analysed by the mind into several parts. Of these the most important are Adoration, Thanksgiving, Penitence, Petition, and Intercession. In this and the following three chapters, some account will be given of these chief kinds of prayer. We begin in this chapter with Adoration and Thanksgiving.

ADORATION

Adoration is loving God for what He is in Himself. It is love looking up like Mary of Bethany sitting at the feet of Jesus; it is love poured out, as when she anointed His feet with the precious perfume. The Scotch catechism says that "the chief end of man is to glorify God and enjoy Him for ever". Man was created to adore, to express reverent admiration, to acknowledge the supreme worth of God. We often come to God because we are in need, it may be of forgiveness, or of some kind of help or deliverance. We love God because we need Him, and for dependent creatures this is right. But although we are never without need, and we glorify God by bringing to Him our need, yet we can also come to God to appreciate His greatness and to give Him our praise.

"We praise thee, we bless thee, we worship thee, we glorify thee, *we give thanks to thee for thy great glory*, O Lord God, heavenly King, God the Father Almighty."

In the spring, a cherry tree in full blossom, wakes our spontaneous admiration and praise. Quite apart from the fruit it may bear later, we rejoice in its beauty, in what it is in itself. We appreciate and love our friends not because they may help us, but for what they are. As Cicero says in his treatise on friendship, "Its whole fruit is in the love itself, for it is not the advantage, procured through a friend, but his love itself that gives delight." So also, because God loves us and we love Him, we find in Him our "chiefest joy". Adoration is giving thanks to God, not for His gifts, but for His great glory. When Isaiah "saw the Lord sitting upon a throne, high and lifted up", he heard the song of the seraphim: "Holy, holy, holy is the Lord of hosts; the whole earth is full of His glory" (Isaiah 6: 3). Aware of the majesty and holiness of God, they adore Him ceaselessly, "with pure seraphic joy". It is this, the highest form of prayer, the chief end of human existence, the very life of heaven, which led Von Hugel to say "religion is adoration".

SOME WAYS OF EXPRESSING ADORATION

Just because adoration is the highest form of prayer, it is, perhaps, for most of us the most difficult. That is not a valid reason for neglecting it until we reach spiritual maturity. Just as in human life love grows by means of the acts which express it, so we learn to adore by adoring. In the Lord's Prayer, Jesus taught us to begin with the adoration of God. It is fitting that a Quiet Time should frequently begin in this way. Here are some ways of expressing Adoration.

I. Adore with your body; kneel down and bow your head. Your body is a part of you; what you do with it has a reflex action on your mind and spirit. "O come, let us worship and *bow* down, let us *kneel* before the Lord our Maker" (Psalm 95: 6). In these familiar words of the Venite, the Psalmist invites us to let our bodies also participate in the worship of God. This is especially helpful on those occasions when we are not "in the mood", do not feel like prayer. Adoration may and often does involve the emotions; but it is also a matter of attitude, intellect, intention and will. All this can be expressed in the posture of the body. To kneel, to bow the head, with the intention of expressing submission, reverence, and awe, is adoration.

II. Think about God and then adore Him in your own words. Call to mind some truth about Him or meditate on one of His attributes—His wisdom, power, holiness, beauty, goodness, truth. Think of Him as revealed in some aspect of creation, or in the life of some hero or saint. Consider Jesus—an aspect of His character, an incident from His life. After thinking for a few moments about God, then express your thoughts in words of love and praise.

III. Use the words of others to adore God. Our own words are often feeble and unworthy; but those who have trodden the pathway of prayer before us, have left words adequate and beautiful, with which we may adore their God and ours. They are found in Holy Scripture, especially the Psalter, and in the hymns and prayers of the Church. It is helpful to commit some of these to memory; then they are always available for use. Don't forget that the Psalter and the Hymnal are the two great aids to adoration. It is an excellent thing to begin a Quiet Time with a psalm or a hymn. The following brief prayers of adoration may be committed to memory.

Glory be to the Father, and to the Son, and to the Holy Ghost; as it was in the beginning, is now, and ever shall be, world without end. Amen.

Holy, holy, holy, Lord God of hosts, heaven and earth are full of Thy glory. Glory be to Thee, O Lord most high. Amen.

Blessed be the Lord, the God of Israel, who alone does wondrous things. Blessed be His glorious name for ever; may His glory fill the whole earth. Amen and Amen.

Blessed art Thou, O Lord, the God of Israel our Father, for ever and ever. Thine, O Lord, is the greatness, and the power, and the glory, and the victory, and the majesty; for all that is in the heavens and the earth is Thine; Thine is the kingdom O Lord, and Thou art exalted as head above all. And now we thank Thee, our God, and praise Thy glorious name. Amen.

Before the glorious throne of Thy majesty, O Lord, and the awful judgement-seat of Thy burning love, we Thy people do kneel with cherubim and seraphim and archangels, worshipping, confessing, and praising Thee, Lord of all, Father, Son, and Holy Spirit for ever. Amen.

THANKSGIVING

Thanksgiving is the grateful acknowledgement of God's gifts. We adore Him for what He is; we give thanks to Him for His benefits. Or do we? One of the worst features of human nature is the tendency to take things for granted. We are all guilty of receiving God's gifts without acknowledgement and gratitude, and He could complain of each one of us "how sharper than a serpent's tooth it is, to have a thankless child". When Christ healed ten lepers "One of them, when he saw that he was healed, turned back, praising God with a loud voice; and he fell on his face at Jesus' feet, giving Him thanks" (Luke 17: 15, 16). If the other nine were grateful for the gift of health, they did not take the trouble to express it. We are often exhorted in the Bible to remember what God has done for us, to recall what He has given to us.

"Bless the Lord, O my soul; and all that is within me, bless His holy name! Bless the Lord, O my soul, and forget not all His benefits" (Psalm 103: 1, 2).

There are three truths about thanksgiving which it is helpful to keep in mind.

I. It is not sufficient to give thanks in general for all the gifts of God; it should be done in particular, in detail. Deliberately recall gifts, experiences, benefits, joys, and then give thanks for this and this and that, telling the Lord explicitly what it is for which you are grateful. The advice of the old hymn is sound: "Count your many blessings, name them *one by one*; and it will surprise you what the Lord has done." One excellent way of doing this is to make a review of the past day during the evening Quiet Time. Try to recall all the good things you have received during that one day, and then thank God for each one of them. At morning prayer thank God for all the gifts of the previous day, the mercies of the past night, the expected blessings of the coming day. Morning and evening—for "it is good to give thanks to the Lord, to sing praises to Thy name, O Most High; to declare Thy steadfast love in the morning, and Thy faithfulness by night" (Psalm 92: 1, 2).

II. Make a habit of giving thanks for everything. Our natural tendency is to confine the expression of gratitude to the pleasures and joys of life, to give thanks only for happy events and favourable circumstances. The Apostle Paul writes, "give thanks in *all* circumstances; for this is the will of God in Christ Jesus for you" (I Thessalonians 5: 18). When he and Silas, having been flogged, were put into the inner prison at Philippi, at midnight they sang hymns to God. The gratitude of the true Christian does not depend on favourable circumstances, for "we know that in everything God works for good with those who love Him, who are called according to His purpose" (Romans 8 : 28). It is not easy, but it is possible to thank God for trials and disappointments, for hardships and sufferings. Accept life as a whole with gratitude, knowing that everything can be used or transformed by the power of God.

III. Two beneficial results of thanksgiving may be mentioned here, by way of encouragement. When a gift of God is received by man with thanksgiving, it is thereby consecrated, it becomes holy to the Lord. Take, for example, the excellent habit of "saying grace" before meals. "Everything created by God is good, and nothing is to be rejected if it is received with thanksgiving; for then it is consecrated by the word of God and prayer" (I Timothy 4 : 4, 5). Food and all the other gifts "which God created to be received with thanksgiving by those who believe and know the truth", are consecrated when acknowledged with thanksgiving and used with gratitude. This is also one of the open secrets of happiness. True, we do not give thanks in order to be happy; but it is a by-product. This is an age in which many people are subject to depression. The cure for this spiritual malady is to establish the habit of daily thanksgiving. "If anyone would tell you the shortest, surest way to all happiness, and all perfection, he must tell you to make a rule to yourself, to thank and praise God for everything that happens to you. For it is certain that whatever seeming calamity happens to you, if you thank and praise God for it, you turn it into a blessing. Could you therefore work miracles, you could not do more for yourself than by this thankful spirit; for it heals with a word and turns all that it touches into happiness."[1]

THE SCOPE OF THANKSGIVING

The wide scope of Christian gratitude may be illustrated by quoting the Prayer of General Thanksgiving from the *Book of Common Prayer*.

Almighty God, Father of all mercies, we, Thine unworthy servants, do give Thee most humble and hearty thanks for all Thy goodness and lovingkindness to us and to all men. We

[1] *A Serious Call to a Devout and Holy Life*—William Law.

bless Thee for our creation, preservation, and all the blessings of this life; but above all, for Thine inestimable love in the redemption of the world by our Lord Jesus Christ; for the means of grace and for the hope of glory. And, we beseech Thee, give us that due sense of all Thy mercies, that our hearts may be unfeignedly thankful; and that we show forth Thy praise, not only with our lips, but in our lives, by giving up ourselves to Thy service, and by walking before Thee in holiness and righteousness all our days, through Jesus Christ our Lord, to whom, with Thee and the Holy Ghost, be all honour and glory, world without end. Amen.

In this great prayer, we express our thanksgiving to God for all His gifts in the two realms of nature and of grace. Let us consider these in turn.

I. We are to give thanks to God "for our creation, preservation, and all the blessings of this life". And I am to give thanks not just for His gifts to me, or to my family and friends, or to the local Church, but for His "goodness and lovingkindness to us and to *all* men". I am to be grateful for what God has given to others and for all that He is doing for them. It is helpful to make a plan of thanksgiving for "all the blessings of this life", so that nothing is left out. The following plan, or something like it, may be used for the seven days of any one week.

NATURE. The creation and preservation of the universe— the wonders of the world—the fertile earth—the sea—the beauty of nature—day and night—the seasons—plants and flowers—birds and animals—the joys of the open air.

HOME AND FAMILY. Parents—children—husband or wife— brothers—sisters—relatives—our house and its amenities— joys and duties of family life.

PEOPLE. Intimate friends—old friends—new friends— acquaintances—neighbours—those I have been enabled to help—all who help me and love me.

DAILY WORK. My job—the strength and skill to do it—the products of my work—fellow-workers—for all workers—the blessings I enjoy through the work of others.

RECREATION.   Leisure—sport—hobbies—books—music— radio—television—for all those who entertain me—holidays.

COUNTRY. Legacy of the past—freedom—just laws—good

institutions—the Queen—ministers of state—all public servants—local council—my town or locality—science—art—education—other nations—the United Nations.

MYSELF. My creation—my body, health and strength—daily food—clothing—shelter—memory—reason—affections—imagination—lessons I have learned—what I have been enabled to do—recent gifts and blessings.

II. We are also to give thanks to God for His "inestimable love in the redemption of the world by our Lord Jesus Christ; for the means of grace and for the hope of glory". Of course it is not possible to draw a line between the order of nature and that of grace. The one Lord is both Creator and Redeemer. The universe itself is a sacrament; the life, power and love of God are mediated through persons and actions and things. Yet although grace works through and transforms nature, we may not identify the two. Jesus Christ has come from heaven and has given to us eternal life. We are to thank God for Him, for the great deliverance wrought by Him, for all the means by which He comes to us, and for the hope of everlasting life. Here is one suggested way of doing this. If the former plan is used in the mornings, this may be used in the evenings—or for an alternative week.

THE INCARNATION OF OUR LORD. The Holy Scriptures—biblical scholars and teachers—Bible Societies—Christian writers and literature.

THE LIFE AND MINISTRY OF OUR LORD. Teachers in university, college and school—doctors, nurses, medical missionaries—social and welfare workers.

THE PASSION AND DEATH OF OUR LORD. For the benefits of His sacrifice, forgiveness, cleansing, moral power, purpose, fellowship, salvation—for all who suffer for Christ's sake.

THE RESURRECTION OF OUR LORD. His abiding presence—the Church Universal—my own Communion—my local Church—for Christians, especially . . .

THE ASCENSION AND PRIESTHOOD OF OUR LORD. For Christ our King, Mediator and Intercessor—for His royal priesthood on earth—clergy and ministers—my own priest or pastor—missionaries—the world mission of the Church.

THE HOLY SPIRIT. For His help, guidance and comfort—for His light, life and holiness—for the fruits and gifts of the Spirit in Christians, especially . . . For the Sacraments of Baptism and the Eucharist.

THE SECOND ADVENT OF OUR LORD. The resurrection of the body—the life everlasting—the Communion of Saints—the Saints—the Saints of our own land—my own dear departed.

SUMMARY

I. Adoration is loving, praising and enjoying God Himself.

II. Adoration may be expressed by the body; by thinking about God and putting our thoughts into words; by using Psalms, Hymns and the Prayers of others.

III. Thanksgiving is the grateful acknowledgement of God's gifts.

IV. We should give thanks not only in general, but also for particular gifts, not only for the pleasures and joys, but also for the sorrows and sufferings of life.

V. Thanksgiving has two beneficial results; it consecrates all gifts and is the surest way to all happiness.

VI. We should give thanks for all the blessings of this life and for the redemption of the world by our Lord Jesus Christ.

CHAPTER EIGHT

SELF-EXAMINATION, CONFESSION AND PARDON

THE MAN GOD ACCEPTS

THERE is a parable of Christ about two men who went up into the temple to pray. The one, a Pharisee, stood and congratulated himself on his many virtues and achievements. "God, I thank Thee that I am not like other men, extortioners, unjust, adulterers, or even like this tax collector. I fast twice a week, I give tithes of all that I get." The other, the tax collector "standing far off, would not even lift up his eyes to heaven, but beat his breast, saying, 'God, be merciful to me a sinner!'" Then follows the comment of Christ. "I tell you, this man went down to his house justified rather than the other; for everyone who exalts himself will be humbled, but he who humbles himself will be exalted." (Luke 18: 9–14). Both men alike were sinful. The Pharisee was unaware of his true condition; his pride was a barrier, his self-righteousness kept him from God. The tax collector was conscious of his sin and frankly acknowledged it. We are all sinners; to know and confess this is essential if we are to approach God and be accepted by Him. In the pattern prayer, Jesus taught us to pray "forgive us our trespasses". This awareness of sin, together with the frank and sorrowful acknowledgement of it to God, is known as penitence or contrition. Penitence involves three things—facing up to our sin through self-examination, confessing it to God, and asking for and receiving His pardon. We shall consider these aspects in turn.

SELF-EXAMINATION

"Let a man examine himself." Before I can honestly confess my sin to God, I must frankly face up to it in myself. I must look within, searching my heart, not shrinking back from a thorough self-examination. Usually the best *time* to do this is at the beginning of the evening prayer period. Quietly review the past day in order to recall any mistakes, faults, negligences and sins within it. The end of the week, the Saturday evening Quiet Time, is also an appropriate occasion on which to make a thorough self-examination. The sins of the past week are confessed and forgiveness is received, in preparation for the worship of the Lord's Day.

Pray for the help of the Holy Spirit before self-examination. We can so easily deceive ourselves, ignoring "the weightier matters of the law" while exaggerating moral trivialities into cardinal sins. True self-knowledge is the gift of God, who alone can supply the insight, the perspective, the sincerity of purpose. It is helpful to memorise and use the following prayer from Psalm 139.

> Search me, O God, and know my heart! Try me and know my thoughts! And see if there be any wicked way in me, and lead me in the way everlasting!

SINS OF OMISSION AND COMMISSION

In preparing a confession, it is well to keep in mind the difference between *sins of omission* and sins of commission. This distinction is well brought out in the General Confession of the *Book of Common Prayer*. "We have left undone the things that we ought to have done, and we have done the things that we ought not to have done." It does not follow that our lives are blameless because we have done nothing wrong. Having done nothing may itself be our sin. Our gravest sins often are omissions—the word of encouragement left unspoken, the opportunity missed, the work neglected, the duty shirked, the helpful deed left undone. In the parable of the Last Judgement, the wicked are condemned for their omissions. "I was hungry and you gave me no food, I was thirsty and you gave me no drink, I was a stranger and you did not welcome me, naked and you did not clothe me, sick and in prison and you did not visit me" (Matthew 25: 42, 43). Of course there is a limit to the number of good works and loving deeds possible in any one day. But it is usually obvious when our omissions have been deliberate and are blameworthy.

Sins of commission may be divided into sins of thought, word, and deed. We cannot always prevent evil thoughts or desires entering the mind, and being tempted is not in itself sin. We are, however, often guilty of deliberately entertaining or harbouring evil in the mind. As for our words, the Apostle Paul provides us in a sentence with a dual test—"speaking the truth in love" (Ephesians 4 : 15). Have my words been true? Have they all been kind? Evil deeds, if recent, are hardly ever difficult to recall and recognise; they are overt, concrete, definite, unmistakable. "For I know my transgressions, and my sin is ever before me" (Psalm 51 : 3). It is not necessary to probe and hunt for evil deeds; it is sufficient to confess those which come almost effortlessly to mind.

CHRIST OUR STANDARD

There is a *positive standard* by which we can measure our lives—the teaching and deeds, the life and character of Jesus Christ. That is why the reading of the New Testament and the Gospels in particular, provides the necessary background for Christian self-examination. It is in the light of Christ that we best see ourselves; and that does not drive us to despair precisely because we are seeing Christ in His mercy and love. As it is put in a well-known prayer: "In the light of the sacrifice of Thy Son upon the cross, we see and acknowledge the hatefulness of our sins; grant us, in that light also to see Thy great and wondrous mercy." When a longer period is being devoted to self-examination, it is helpful to use an incident or passage from the Gospels or Epistles as background. There are four passages in the New Testament which are widely used for this purpose:

The two Commandments of Love—Mark 12 : 28–34.
The Beatitudes, Christ's eight-fold description of Christian character—Matthew 5 : 1–12.
The Hymn in praise of Love—I Corinthians 13.
The nine Fruits of the Spirit—Galatians 5 : 22, 23.

The use of a positive standard, helps to save us from two dangers associated with the habit of self-examination. It is possible to become excessively introspective, to become too interested in one's own moral condition, to become morbidly obsessed with sin. John Bunyan came to recognise that one of the devices of the devil was to keep him always thinking of his sins. That is almost as bad as never to think of them at all! There is also the danger of scrupulosity, of making molehills into mountains, moral trifles into grave sins. It is so easy to lose all sense of perspective "straining out a gnat and swallowing a camel". The Jews, in order to avoid ceremonial defilement refused on Good Friday morning, to enter the palace of Pilate. "They were demanding the crucifixion of the Lord of Glory, but of course no one thought of that as defilement; to enter the heathen ruler's house would be defilement."[1] If we are to keep a sense of proportion, if we are to have a sense of what is vital, we need a standard of reference. If we keep looking at Christ, we shall overcome these dangers of looking within. We must not attempt to avoid them by refusing to look within; the perils of the unexamined life are far greater.

THE CONFESSION OF SIN

After self-examination, confession. Having faced up to our sin, we own up to God. The Psalmist says: "I acknowledged my sin *to Thee*, and I did not hide my iniquity; I said, 'I will confess my transgressions to the Lord'; then Thou didst forgive the guilt of my sin" (Psalm 32: 5). Having examined yourself, then kneel down, think of the Saviour on the cross, lift up your heart to Him now interceding in heaven, and tell God all about your sin. Personal confession should be *specific and definite*. In public worship, as is appropriate, we join with others in a general confession of sin. But in private prayer that is not sufficient. Tell God exactly what it was that you thought, said or did, or neglected to do. Not "I have been untruthful"; but "I told A.B. I had climbed Snowdon, when in fact I turned back long before reaching the summit". Not "I have neglected my duty"; but "I went for a walk in the country last Sunday afternoon, instead of visiting my grandfather in hospital". Confess the evil in the precise form in which it was manifested. On the other hand, confession is not just the acknowledgement of sins. Our sins (in the plural) are like the surface symptons of a disease; they are the fruit of sin. I *do* evil because I *am* evil. Real contrition, deep penitence involves

[1] *Readings in St. John's Gospel*—William Temple.

this acknowledgement. My sin, as distinct from sins, is my pride, self-will, self-centredness; rebellion against God, alienation from God, making myself rather than God the centre of the world. In confessing sins let us also acknowledge the sinfulness from which they spring. Furthermore, our sin is not only personal, it is also *corporate*. Listen to this confession of the prophet Isaiah. "Woe is me! For I am lost; for I am a man of unclean lips, and I dwell in the midst of a people of unclean lips" (Isaiah 6: 5). I, unclean—a people unclean. We are all bound together in the bundle of life, and my own sins and sinfulness have contributed to the social, national, racial sin. I am, for example, a part of that world in which there are many millions of refugees, and of hungry, starving people. This is one reason why an individual should confess his sins together with others, as in corporate worship. Even when confessing in private, it is sometimes better to say "we" rather than "I". "Forgive us *our* trespasses" is to be prayed by an individual in his own room (Matthew 6: 6 and 9). These three truths about confession are complimentary—it should be both particular and general, both personal and corporate, a confession of sins and of sin.

THE CONDITIONS OF FORGIVENESS

In the moving story of the vision and call of Isaiah, there is a three-fold sequence (Isaiah 6: 1–7). "I saw the Lord"; first comes the vision of God in all His majesty and holiness. "And I said, woe is me"; the confession of personal sin is the result of the vision of the Divine holiness. Only as we become aware of God can we become aware of our own sinfulness. "Your guilt is taken away, your sin forgiven." Having confessed his sin, the prophet is cleansed, and hears the Divine declaration of pardon. Without this action of God, the confession of man would be of no avail. For confession does not of itself bring cleansing and forgiveness, although it must precede that Divine act. And so after confession, ask for and take the pardon of God.

The conditions for receiving God's pardon are set forth clearly in the New Testament.

I. Forgiveness is offered to all those who forgive their brethren. In the Lord's Prayer, Jesus taught us to say "forgive us

our trespasses, *as we forgive* them that trespass against us".
This is the only petition in the prayer which Christ singled out
for comment. "For if you forgive men their trespasses, your
heavenly Father also will forgive you; but if you do not forgive
men their trespasses, neither will your Father forgive your
trespasses" (Matthew 6: 14, 15). He who refuses forgiveness
to others, cannot himself be forgiven. Conversely, he who has
been forgiven much by God, must himself forgive his neighbour (Matthew 18: 23–35).

II. Forgiveness is offered to all those who confess their sins.
"If we say we have no sin, we deceive ourselves and the truth
is not in us. If we confess our sins, He is faithful and just, and
will forgive our sins and cleanse us from all unrighteousness"
(I John 1: 8, 9).

III. Forgiveness is offered to all those who repent. Repentance is not remorse, nor is it necessarily accompanied by
strong emotion, though it frequently is. It is a change of mind,
an act of will; the deliberate turning from self and sin to God
and goodness. "Repent therefore and *turn* again; that your
sins may be blotted out" (The Acts 3: 19).

IV. Forgiveness is offered to all those who have faith. It
can never be merited or earned by man; is not a right we can
claim from God. It is possible only through the sacrifice of
Christ, who "died that we might be forgiven", and lives for
ever to make intercession for us. "If any one does sin, we have
an advocate with the Father, Jesus Christ the righteous; and
He is the expiation for our sins" (I John 2: 1, 2).

RECEIVING GOD'S FORGIVENESS

It is very important that we should actually ask for and take
the forgiveness of God. Having fulfilled the conditions, we
can do this with humble assurance on the ground of His
promises. His promises—not my feelings. Whether or not I
feel forgiven is irrelevant. "If Thou O Lord, shouldst mark
iniquities, Lord, who could stand? But there is forgiveness
with Thee, that Thou mayest be feared. I wait for the Lord,
my soul waits, and *in His word* I hope" (Psalm 130: 3–5).
Some find it helpful to receive His forgiveness by a symbolic
act, such as lifting up the hands to take it. In asking for pardon
it may also be helpful to use words hallowed by the long

tradition of public worship. The following is an adaptation and expansion of the absolution from the Service of Holy Communion in the *Book of Common Prayer*.

Almighty God, heavenly Father, who of Thy great mercy has promised forgiveness to all who forgive their brethren, confess their sins, and with hearty repentance and true faith turn unto Thee; have mercy upon me; pardon and deliver me from all my sins; confirm and strengthen me in all goodness, and bring me to eternal life; through my Saviour and Advocate Jesus Christ. Amen.

Having received God's pardon and absolution, we should put the sin confessed and forgiven completely behind our backs. "I, I am He who blots out your transgression for my own sake, and I will not remember your sins" (Isaiah 43 : 25). If God no longer remembers our sins, why should we, being forgiven, remember them? Let the experience of Christian in *Pilgrim's Progress* be ours. "So I saw in my dream, that just as Christian came up with the cross, his burden loosed from off his shoulders, and fell from off his back, and began to tumble; and so continued to do, till it came to the mouth of the sepulchre, where it fell in, *and I saw it no more.*"

SUMMARY

I. God rejects the proud and accepts the penitent.

II. Penitence means facing up to sin through self-examination, confessing it to God, and asking His forgiveness for it.

III. The best time for self-examination, which should be preceded by a prayer for the help of the Holy Spirit, is at the end of a day or week.

IV. We should confess the good things we have neglected to do, as well as our sins of thought, word and deed.

V. Christ is the standard by which we should examine our lives.

VI. Our confession, whether of sins or of sin, should be both particular and general, personal and corporate.

VII. There are four conditions for receiving God's forgiveness: the forgiveness of others, the confession of sin, repentance toward God and faith in the Lord Jesus Christ.

VIII. God's forgiveness should be received with complete assurance on the ground of His promises.

CHAPTER NINE

PETITION

AN excellent way of understanding God, is to think of Him in terms of the best and highest in our human relationships. We must take care not to be misled by the use of analogy. God is unlike as well as like us. Even when at our very best, He is in some respects like us, we have to add "how much more". Yet in spite of these dangers, Christ Himself taught us to think of prayer as analogous to the relationship between a father and his children. An essential element in such a relationship is asking. Children ask for things; even imperfect parents respond by giving good things. "What man of you, if his son asks him for a loaf, will give him a stone? Or if he asks for a fish, will give him a serpent? If you then, who are evil, know how to give good gifts to your children, how much more will your Father who is in heaven give good things to those who ask Him?" (Matthew 7: 9–11).

PRAYERS OF ASKING

Prayer in which we ask God for something is called petition. With reference to this element in prayer, people are apt to go to one of two extremes. There are those for whom this one colour is the whole rainbow. Prayer is asking God for things—just that and nothing else. This is often the unexamined assumption of the natural man. Prayer is not understood as fellowship with God, a personal communion, which like a jewel has many facets. There is no appreciation of adoration and thanksgiving, of penitence and offering, of listening and co-operation with God. Whenever prayer is thus misunderstood exclusively in terms of asking, almost inevitably it becomes self-centred. Man tries to use God for the achievement of his own purposes. In reaction against this narrow and selfish conception of prayer, there is a tendency to swing to the other extreme of refusing to ask at all. "I will seek God solely for His own sake, that I may live in fellowship with Him, and offer to Him my worship and obedience". Such a view of prayer seems, at first sight, to be more spiritual and high-minded. Two considerations, however, will suffice to show that such is not the case.

If prayer at its best is fellowship with God, then we may take the analogy of our relationships with one another in human life. Have we any experience of fellowship in which asking and receiving have no place at all? Would the relationship between parents and children be "higher", if asking and giving were eliminated? Is friendship selfish because one friend requests something of the other? Is it not rather enriched by the right kind of asking and receiving? Much more convincing to the Christian, however, is the example and the teaching of Jesus Christ. Jesus asked God for things, both for Himself and for others. In His sayings and parables about prayer, the element of petition is conspicuous and indeed predominant. There can be no "higher" prayer than that practised and taught by Christ—and that includes petition. Prayer *is* fellowship with God; a fellowship of giving and receiving, of asking and taking.

THE LAWS OF PRAYER

"Ask, and it will be given you; seek, and you will find; knock, and it will be opened to you. For everyone who asks receives, and he who seeks finds, and to him who knocks it will be opened" (Luke 11: 9, 10). Here Christ states a fundamental truth about prayer, without any reservations or qualifications. This is in full accord with His customary method of teaching. He was not like a scientist or a logician, making carefully balanced factual statements about abstract truth. He taught as a poet, appealing to the imagination, presenting one truth at a time, with full depth and force. The necessary qualifications are supplied at other times, when He is concerned with other aspects of the truth. Those who ask, receive; but they must ask in accordance with certain laws, there are necessary conditions which must be fulfilled. What are they?

PRAYING IN HARMONY WITH THE MIND OF CHRIST

Our petitions, to be effective, must be offered *in Christ's name*. "Whatever you ask in My name, I will do it that the

Father may be glorified in the Son; if you ask anything in My name, I will do it" (John 14: 13). This does not mean that if we tag the name of Jesus Christ on to the end of our petitions, and finish up all our prayers with the magic formula, "this we ask through Jesus Christ our Lord", they will be granted! In the Bible "the name" means the nature; it stands for the person as known, his revealed character. To pray in Christ's name is to pray in accordance with His nature and character, in harmony with His revealed will and purpose. That is why He can say: "Truly, truly, I say to you, if you ask anything of the Father, He will give it to you in My name; ask, and you will receive, that your joy may be full" (John 16: 23, 24). The disciples had always prayed as devout Jews, from now on they would be able to pray according to the mind of the Master. "If you abide in Me, and My words abide in you, ask whatever you will, and it shall be done for you" (John 15: 7). In the teaching of Christ—"My words"—we have the mind of Christ; as a result, whatever we ask is granted (see also John 15: 16). This then is the basic condition for effective petition—it must be according to Christ, in harmony with His revealed character and purpose.

PRAYING WITH FAITH

Our petitions must be offered in *faith*. We must pray to God with confidence in His perfect wisdom, power, and love. Human parents, though tainted with evil, know how to give good gifts to their children. "How much more will your Father in heaven, give good things to those who ask Him?" (Matthew 7: 11). We are to approach Him with this sure confidence, with this serene faith. Such trust is possible because Jesus Christ has revealed God as trustworthy. Even as we pray, we are to believe that God is already answering. "Therefore I tell you, whatever you ask in prayer, believe that you receive it, and you will" (Mark 11: 24). James, the brother of the Lord, underlines this condition for effective prayer. "Let him ask in faith, with no doubting, for he who doubts is like a wave of the sea that is driven and tossed by the wind. For that person must not suppose that a double-minded man, unstable in all his ways, will receive anything from the Lord" (James 1: 6, 7).

PRAYING WITH PERSEVERANCE

Our petitions must be *persistent*. To urge upon His disciples this duty of perseverance in prayer, Christ told two parables. A householder is in the embarrassing position of having no food to set before an unexpected guest. At midnight he goes and knocks on the door of a friend, who, being in bed with his family, is unwilling to rise, and give him the three loaves for which he is asking. Then follows Christ's own comment on the situation. "I tell you, though he will not get up and give him anything because he is his friend, yet because of his importunity he will rise and give him whatever he needs" (Luke 11 : 5–10). In the second parable a defenceless widow keeps on coming to a judge for arbitration and justice. Having no respect for either God or man, he at first refuses to vindicate her. Later on he says, "Because this widow bothers me, I will vindicate her, or she will wear me out by her continual coming" (Luke 18 : 1–8). These are not parables of comparison but of contrast. God, who is altogether *unlike* the lazy householder and the unjust judge, will certainly answer those who persist in prayer. Perseverance is necessary because of delay, and the purpose of delay is to strengthen faith. "Keep on asking, and it will be given you."

PRAYING WITH CHARITY

Our petitions must be offered *in charity*. God will not hear the prayers of those whose relationships with their fellow-men are unjust and uncharitable. "When you spread forth your hands, I will hide My eyes from you; even though you make many prayers, I will not listen; your hands are full of blood. Wash yourselves; make yourselves clean; remove the evil of your doings from before My eyes; cease to do evil, learn to do good; seek justice, correct oppression; defend the fatherless, plead for the widow" (Isaiah 1 : 15–17). Like Isaiah and other Hebrew prophets, Christ insists upon justice, mercy, and faithfulness in our personal relationships, and condemns the hypocrisy of those who devour widows' houses and for a pretence make long prayers (Matthew 23 : 14, 23). If I have quarrelled with my brother, or if he is justly offended with me, my worship is unacceptable. "First be reconciled to your brother, and then come and offer your gift" (Matthew 5 : 23, 24). I must be in love and charity with all men, when I pray. "And whenever you stand praying, forgive, if you have anything against anyone; so that your Father also who is in heaven may forgive you your trespasses." (Mark 11 : 25). To be in right relationship with God, one must be in right relationship with men; acceptable prayers ascend from just and charitable hearts. These, then, are the necessary conditions or requirements, if we are to receive that for which we ask. We are to pray in harmony with His mind and purpose, and with faith, persistence, and charity. If we ask in obedience to these laws, we shall receive.

PETITION AND CHARACTER

We have just seen that if our petitions are to be answered, they must be offered in Christ's name. If we are to receive, then we must ask in accordance with the mind of Christ, in harmony with the will of God. But what is the will of God for us? It is primarily that we should be like Jesus Christ in character. The world is "a vale of soul making"; it is the purpose of God that we should *be* persons of a certain kind, Christ-like persons. God is not *primarily* concerned with what we *do*, but with what we *are* and may *become*. As the Apostle Paul expressed it: "My little children, with whom I am again in travail until Christ be formed in you!" (Galatians 4 : 19). It is God's purpose that we should be "conformed to the image of His Son"; prayer according to His purpose is then prayer for *that*—for Christlikeness. This should be the burden, the primary concern of our petitions. That is why the great Christian supplications are for qualities of character. We are encouraged to pray for "the fruits of the Spirit which are the virtues of Christ". Take, for example, this concise collect:

Almighty and everlasting God, give unto us the increase of faith, hope, and charity; and, that we may obtain that which Thou dost promise, make us to love that which Thou dost command; through Jesus Christ our Lord.

Here our petition is that the three great Christian virtues or graces, faith, hope, and love, may increase in us, and that we may love that which God has commanded. In our prayers of supplication for qualities of character, it is important to be positive, to concentrate on the virtues or graces we need. It is easy to get into the bad habit of praying about faults, weaknesses, and vices. "Please, Lord, help me to overcome my bad temper." In the very act of praying, I am preoccupied with a vice. How much better to pray: "Please, Lord, grant to me the patience of Christ and the fruit of the Spirit which is self-control." This is one of the great advantages of reading the Bible, especially the New Testament, in a Quiet Time. Looking first at the Lord Jesus, the petitions which are suggested by the Bible reading and meditation, will be for those virtues and graces which we see in Him.

THE SCOPE OF PETITION

If we pray in accordance with the principles taught by Christ, and with the primary concern of becoming like Him in character, then we need have no hesitation in praying about everything. "Have no anxiety about anything, but in *everything* by prayer and supplication with thanksgiving let your requests be made known to God" (Philippians 4 : 6). We need to be on our guard against the widespread tendency to divide life into the material and the spiritual, and the assumption that it is right to pray only for things spiritual. Such a division is unbiblical. God is not concerned with a special area of life labelled "spiritual" or "religious"; He is the Lord of all life. All that concerns us is of concern to Him, and may be brought to Him in prayer. For example, to pray for money or for a car, if you are in real need of them, is just as spiritual as to pray for consolation in bereavement, or for courage to face danger. Nor is it right to exclude the small or the trivial, and to confine our petitions to matters of moment or importance. We are not always in a position to say what is trivial. Certainly it is better to bring needs rather than wants to God. What we want may not be what we need, and may be contrary to God's will and to human welfare. On the other hand, it does not follow that a thing is wrong because it is wanted. Why assume that the will of God is necessarily unpleasant! Unless our wants are clearly contrary to the will of God, they may be included in our prayers, subject to that will. Pray about everything that concerns you, leaving the answer with complete assurance to Him, who is perfect wisdom, power, and love. Not that God leaves us, if we trust Him, to our own thoughts and desires. "God is at work in you, both to will and to work for His good pleasure" (Philippians 2: 13). The Holy Spirit within teaches us how to pray. This is how Lady Julian of Norwich put this truth into the mouth of God.

> I am the ground of thy beseeching.
> First, it is My will that thou have it,
> And then I make thee to will it,
> And then I make thee to beseech it,
> And if thou beseech it, how should it then be that thou should not have thy beseeching?

We do well to ask for this help of God in offering all our petitions.

Let Thy merciful ears, O Lord, be open to the prayers of Thy humble servants; and that they may obtain their petitions make them to ask such things as shall please Thee; through Jesus Christ our Lord.

SUMMARY

I. Not all prayer is petition; but petition is an essential part of prayer, as is evident in the teaching and example of Christ.

II. There are certain necessary conditions or requirements if we are to receive that for which we ask.

III. Our petitions must be in harmony with the mind of Christ.

IV. We must pray with confidence.

V. When faced with delay or difficulty, we must persevere.

VI. When praying, we must be in right relationships with our fellow-men.

VII. We should pray primarily for qualities of character, for the virtues of Christ.

VIII. All that is of concern to us may be included in our petitions.

CHAPTER TEN

INTERCESSION

WHICH of you who has a friend will go to him at midnight and say to him, "Friend, lend me three loaves; for a friend of mine has arrived on a journey, and I have nothing to set before him." Why did the householder in this familiar parable beg for the three loaves? He was not knocking for himself, he was not asking for bread to satisfy his own hunger. He kept on knocking and asking on behalf of another, the unexpected guest, "a friend of mine". Asking for oneself is petition; asking on behalf of another is intercession. It has been truly said that "the greatest thing you can do for any man, is to pray for him". Why should we pray for others? After considering the incentive, we shall then go on to describe the methods.

LOVE ON ITS KNEES

Dr. H. E. Fosdick has described intercession as "love on its knees". The householder in Christ's parable was concerned that his unexpected guest should have something to eat. Concerned! "I couldn't care less!" If that had been his attitude, he would not have gone hammering on the door of a neighbour at midnight, persevering until he got what his guest needed. We shall knock on God's door, if we really care for others, and are deeply concerned about their needs. The patriarch Abraham kept on interceding for the wicked city of Sodom, even at the risk of presumption, only because he cared for the city, or at least for a possible righteous nucleus of people within it (Genesis 18 : 22 to 33). Notice also the intercession of Moses for the idolatrous Hebrews. "But now, if Thou wilt forgive their sin—and if not, blot me, I pray Thee, out of Thy book which Thou hast written" (Exodus 32: 32). So great is his love for the people, that he is willing to perish with them, though innocent, rather than live without them. Such a love drove him to his knees. The Lord Jesus when He "knew that His hour had come to depart out of this world to the Father,

67

having loved His own who were in the world, He loved them to the end" (John 13: 1). As an expression of that love, He offered up the great prayer of intercession for His friends, the most fully recorded prayer of Jesus, before laying down His life on their behalf (John 17). But He did not confine intercession to the circle of His friends. He practised His own precept, "love your enemies and pray for those who persecute you" (Matthew 5: 44). As He was being nailed to the cross, He was praying "Father, forgive them; for they know not what they do" (Luke 23: 34). Love intercedes. He who cares for others, prays for others.

METHODS USELESS WITHOUT LOVE

We can see here the intimate relationship between prayer and life. Intercession is not primarily a matter of method, of "know how". Methods or plans of intercession without love, are about as useful as a locomotive without steam. Love is the motive, caring the incentive. The saying "he prayeth best who loveth best" applies especially to intercession. We fail here, not just because of a lack of time or even because of intellectual difficulties about prayer. "The chief obstacles to intercession are moral. We live for what we can get; our dominant desires are selfish. The main current of our lives runs in the channel of our ambitions, and our thoughts of other people and of great causes are but occasional eddies on the surface of the stream."[1] Learning to intercede is learning to love. Must we then wait until we love others sufficiently before we start praying for them? This is a version of the old query "which comes first, the chicken or the egg?" It is not a case of first this and then that. Love and intercession belong together. Love a person and, given a belief in prayer, you will pray for him; pray for him and you will love him more. Intercession is one way, it may be the greatest way of obeying the commandment, "you shall love your neighbour as yourself".

PRAYING FOR INDIVIDUALS

Intercession has been described as "prayer with names in it". Aaron the high-priest was commanded to wear a breast-
[1] *The Meaning of Prayer*—H. E. Fosdick.

piece on which were inscribed the names of the twelve patri-archs. "So Aaron shall bear the names of the sons of Israel in the breastpiece of judgement upon his heart, when he goes into the holy place, to bring them to continual remembrance before the Lord" (Exodus 28: 29). We also are to go into the presence of God bearing names. What names? It is obviously impossible to pray for all the individuals on earth, and hardly possible, for most of us, to pray for all the individuals we know. This is not required of us. Just as in life, I have the opportunity and the obligation of helping some, and could not possibly help all; so I have the responsibility of praying for some and not for all. Obviously a man should pray for the members of his own family, for personal friends, for all who are "near and dear", for fellow-workers, for acquaintances who are sick or in need. But in addition, God often gives to us what the Quakers would call "a concern" for this person or that. A certain individual keeps coming to mind, and there is an aware-ness of special responsibility for him. It is an excellent thing to make a list of all the individuals for whom we ought to pray. There is an old Chinese proverb to the effect that "the strongest memory is weaker than the palest ink". Such a list ensures that no one is forgotten. It should be revised from time to time, both by the addition of new names, and the omission of those for whom we no longer have a special responsibility.

HOW TO PRAY FOR A PERSON

How should one intercede for a person? Is it sufficient to say "God bless John Smith" and leave it at that? Hardly! Don't start praying right away. Spend just a few moments thinking about John Smith, about his present circumstances and needs. Then bring him into the presence of the Lord, just as the four men in the gospel story carried the paralytic into the presence of Christ. Lastly, pray for him. Whether or not you know his needs, remember that the primary purpose of your petition, is that he should know and do the will of God, should become more like Jesus Christ, should fulfil God's purpose. Pray this for him in your own words, or by using the great prayers vicariously. Here are two examples of what is meant—the one a collect, the other St. Paul's prayer for the Christians at Ephesus.

Lord of all power and might, who art the author and giver of all good things: graft in the heart of John Smith the love of Thy name, increase in him true religion, nourish him with all goodness, and of Thy great mercy keep him in the same; through Jesus Christ our Lord.

For John Smith, I bow my knees before Thee, O Father, from whom every family in heaven and on earth is named, that according to the riches of Thy glory, he may be strengthened with might through Thy Spirit in the inner man, and that Christ may dwell in his heart through faith; that he, being rooted and grounded in love, may have power to comprehend with all the saints what is the breadth and length and height and depth, and to know the love of Christ which surpasses knowledge, that he may be filled with all the fullness of God.

PRAYING FOR CAUSES

Although we cannot possibly pray for all people *individually*, yet we can and ought to intercede "for all sorts and conditions of men". This we may do by praying for whole groups of people, especially for groups engaged in some special task, commonly called "causes". Since it is not possible to pray for everything, everyday, it is helpful to make a plan of intercession. This may be for use in the morning or in the evening, or for both. It may be a plan for a week, a fortnight or a month, and may also include the names of individuals from the list suggested in the section above. Here is one such plan for a week.

SUNDAY

The Church Universal.
The Christian Ministry.
My own Local Church.
Local Church Officers, Teachers and Workers.

MONDAY

My Family and Relatives.
Personal Friends.
All Parents, Children and Homes.

TUESDAY

Schools, Colleges and Universities.
Teachers, Speakers, Writers.
Children's and Youth Work.
Scientists, Artists, Sportsmen and Entertainers.

WEDNESDAY

Work-Mates and all Workers.
Employers and Employed.
My Trades Union.
Commerce and Industry.

THURSDAY

The Work of Healing.
Local Hospital and Doctors and Nurses.
The Sick.
The Needy.
The Bereaved.

FRIDAY

Our Country.
Queen and Royal Family.
Ministers of State and Parliament.
Local Government.
The Nations and U.N.O.

SATURDAY

The World Mission of the Church.
Individual Missionaries.
Missionary Societies.
New Converts and Churches.
Unbelievers—Those I am concerned to win.

TWIN DANGERS TO BE AVOIDED

Ulysses had the difficult task of sailing his ship through a narrow strait, midway between the twin monsters, Scylla and Charybdis. To avoid the one was to be in danger of the other. In intercession the two dangers to be avoided are narrowness on the one hand and vague generalities on the other. The man who prayed:

> God bless me and my wife
> My son John and his wife
> Us four—no more—Amen

was obviously guilty of narrow, confined, self-centred, or at best family-centred prayer. There are others besides family and friends who are in need of our prayers, and a Christian should have a global outlook, not a vision which sees no farther than the village pump. But, while avoiding narrowness and the parochial outlook, intercession should not degenerate into vagueness and generalities. What does a man expect to happen when he prays "God bless China"? Such a prayer is like a lens that has never been focused, like an arrow shot anywhere and therefore nowhere. Intercession should be clear, focused, definite, like that of the householder who came at midnight asking for the loaves. He knew exactly what he wanted, including the number—three. One way of avoiding these extremes, and of ensuring that intercession is definite in its objectives and wide in its range, is to pray both for the individual and for the group to which he belongs. While praying for your friend who has emigrated to New Zealand, pray also for the government of that land. When interceding for a missionary in Korea, include the whole Church in that country. If you are praying for someone in hospital, include the other patients and the staff of doctors and nurses. Another way of ensuring that intercession is both definite and wide, is to use a liturgical prayer, such as the General Intercession "for all sorts and conditions of men" with special intentions. Before saying the prayer, tell God the names of the individuals or groups, for whom especially on this occasion you are praying it. In these ways, intercession can be made particular and definite in objective and also truly catholic in range.

OUR TWO HELPERS

Intercession is a special form of petition; it is asking on behalf of others. Therefore all that Christ taught about petition is applicable also to intercession. We must intercede according to the mind of Christ, with faith, with persistence and with charity. By such prayer we co-operate with God for the fulfilment of His purposes in the lives of others and in the world. Intercession is a mysterious but mighty force. The Apostle James says "the prayer of a righteous man has great power in its effects" (James 5: 16). Only those who love deeply, and who share this conviction about the power of intercession, are likely to be faithful in this costly ministry. But it is not a ministry we exercise, or can exercise alone. As Aaron the high-priest went into the sanctuary bearing names for intercession, so Christians now have a great High Priest and Mediator. Jesus Christ, crucified, risen and ascended has entered into the holy place not made with hands and lives for ever to make intercession for us. Pleading the merits of His eternal sacrifice, His powerful prayers avail for us and for all mankind. We come as members of His Body, of the Church which is "a royal priesthood", a community of intercessors, to join our prayers with His, on behalf of all men. We are "in Christ", praying with Him for others. Not only are we interceding with Christ our "Advocate with the Father", but also with the Holy Spirit, our Advocate within. "Likewise the Spirit helps us in our weakness; for we do not know how to pray as we ought, but the Spirit Himself intercedes for us with sighs too deep for words. And He who searches the hearts of men knows what is the mind of the Spirit, because the Spirit intercedes for the Saints according to the will of God" (Romans 8: 26, 27). Both Christ and the Holy Spirit intercede for us. With both Christ above and the Holy Spirit within, we intercede for others. With these Divine Helpers we cannot fail.

SUMMARY

I. Intercession is praying for others.

II. The incentive to intercession is love.

III. We should pray for individuals who are "near and dear" and for those for whom we feel a special concern.

IV. Think first of the needs of the individual, then bring him into the presence of Christ and pray for him.

V. We should also intercede for groups and causes, making use of a plan.

VI. Avoid both narrowness and vagueness; let your intercessions be comprehensive and definite.

VII. We intercede with Jesus Christ above and the Holy Spirit within.

CHAPTER ELEVEN

PRAYING WITH THE WHOLE PERSONALITY

THE GREAT COMMANDMENT

ON one occasion, the Lord Jesus Christ was asked which of the six hundred and thirteen commandments of the Law of Moses came first in importance. He replied: "The Lord our God, the Lord is one; and you shall love the Lord your God with all your heart, and with all your soul, and with all your mind, and with all your strength" (Mark 12: 29, 30). Misguided attempts have sometimes been made to give exact definitions of the words, heart, soul, mind, strength, as if they referred to quite different aspects of the personality. This is not possible, for the Hebrews thought of man as one whole. For example, in the Bible the word "heart" is used of the will, of the intellect and of the emotions. In citing these words, Christ is not using the exact language of a psychologist, but the picture language of a poet. In modern parlance, He is saying: You shall love the Lord your God lock, stock, and barrel—hook, line, and sinker! Man is to love God *with his whole being*. Every facet of his many-sided life, every faculty of his personality is to be involved and engaged in that worship and service, that trust and obedience which is God's due. And what is true of life, is true also of the devotional life.

In the last four chapters, we have been thinking about Adoration, Thanksgiving, Penitence, Petition, and Intercession, stressing the fact that if the devotional life is to be balanced and whole, all these chief kinds of prayer must be included. But this does not of itself ensure that prayer will be full and complete. Not only every kind of prayer, but also every aspect of the personality of the one offering the prayers, should enter into the worship of God. Now a man thinks, feels, and wills. Therefore thought, emotion, and volition should all enter fully into his prayers. Of course, these are not distinct faculties; man is not like a store with separate departments. It may be that all three—thinking, feeling, and willing—

are involved in every experience, in varying degree. It is that variation, however, which is important. In the course of one evening a schoolboy may prove the theorem of Pythagoras, listen to jazz music, and engage in a bout of boxing. In the first, thought; in the second, emotion; in the third, striving, is predominant. In this chapter, we shall study the place of feeling, willing, and thinking in the prayer life, in that order. The body also can share in the worship of God, and consideration will be given to this aspect in the conclusion.

MISTAKING THE PART FOR THE WHOLE

Life without feeling or emotion would be hardly worth living, and devotion would certainly be incomplete without it. If we are to love God whole-heartedly, our feelings must enter into our prayers, our emotions into our worship. But before turning to the positive aspect of this truth, it is necessary first to take note of a common error. It is often assumed that because feeling is a part of prayer, therefore you cannot pray without your feelings. This is rather like the assumption that because petition is a part of prayer, all prayer is petition. It is to mistake the part for the whole. Yet this mistake is widespread, and is usually expressed like this: "I pray only when I feel like it; otherwise it would not be genuine and real." One has only to apply this to other aspects of life to see how absurd it is. On Monday at 6 o'clock in the morning a bus-driver is lying in bed, listening to the horrid noise of his alarum clock. He is due on duty at 7.15 a.m. The morning is cold and foggy, so instead of getting up, he turns over in bed, saying to himself, "I don't think I'll go to work today, I don't exactly feel like it!" Because he is "on duty", he goes irrespective of his feelings. Social life would be impossible if we all acted simply on the basis of inclination. In no sphere of life do we make the discharge of our obligations dependent on our feelings—or, if we do, it is at least recognised as a moral failure. To worship God is to give Him the glory *due* to His name. It is "our bounden duty", the primary obligation of man, to be discharged whether we feel like it or not.

MASTERING OUR MOODS

Even the most devout and saintly person does not always feel in the mood for prayer. Our feelings are by their very nature changing and inconstant. This does not mean that love is inconstant, for love is not only a feeling; it is a sentiment of the whole personality. The love of a good mother for her child is constant. Her feelings for the child vary with the circumstances. At one time she feels tenderness; at another anger. Most of the time, when preoccupied with other things, she has no feeling for the child at all. So also our love for God may be constant; but within that unchanging sentiment feelings come and go, wax and wane. Our feelings rise and fall like the temperature chart of a fever-stricken patient. To depend upon them is like building the house of prayer on shifting sands. What was the very first difficulty encountered by Christian in Pilgrim's Progress, on his way to the Celestial City? He fell into "the Slough of Despond". For some, moods are the first —and sometimes the continuing—great enemy of the prayer life. They can be overcome by making prayer a matter of habit, not of mood, of will, not of feeling. Have appointed times, established habits of prayer, and keep to them whether you feel like it or not. Pray with your feelings if they are spontaneously present, pray without them if they are absent, pray in spite of them if they are contrary. If you hoist the sail of your prayer-boat and no wind of feeling is blowing, get out the oars of the will and row. It is not the case that devotion is of no value, or is of less value, when feeling is absent. When prayer is entirely a matter of will, that resolute intention of the will, that full constancy of purpose, is itself a costly and precious offering to God.

PRAYING WITH THE FEELINGS

We turn now to the complementary truth. It has just been stated that there can be complete devotion although feeling is absent. It would, however, be very far from complete if it were absent *all the time*. We should not allow ourselves to be influenced by the foolish contemporary fashion of disparaging emotion in the religious life. A generation which has gone crazy about sport, by a strange inconsistency, tends to regard enthusiasm for God as suspect, unbalanced, fanatical. To honour reason and the will, and despise the emotions, may be good Stoicism; it has nothing to do with Christianity. Even some Christian writers, while making the valuable point that love (agape) is not a matter of liking and feeling, have gone to the other extreme of supposing that warm-blooded emotion has no place at all in the greatest of all the virtues. They have made love as cold as charity! But true love involves the whole personality, mind, will, and emotion. What human being would like to be the object of a love which was *always* without emotion? There is an emotional warmth and fervour in the devotion of the prophet Hosea, the apostle Paul, Bernard of Clairvaux, Charles Wesley—to mention but a few. Full devotion is suffused with emotion, and, as in human life, it is this which gives warmth, colour, and depth to the relationship with God.

KINDLING THE FIRE

"We cannot kindle when we will
The fire which in the heart resides."

These words of Matthew Arnold may serve as a warning against the attempt to produce emotion, to work up feeling, to stimulate fervour artificially. There is a greater need today, however, of the warning given by St. Paul: "Do not quench the Spirit" (I Thessalonians 5: 19). The worship of the primitive Church was pentecostal. The Spirit who had been outpoured at Pentecost "with a sudden great sound, as it had been a mighty wind, in the likeness of fiery tongues", continued to move in the assembly, and to inspire spontaneous praise, prayer, and utterance. Wind and fire! A plea has already been made for pattern and order in the devotional life. But what use is pattern without power, order without fervour? The Lord does not require a devotion which is "faultily faultless, icily regular, splendidly null".[1] The Spirit who moves and teaches us to pray is like wind and fire. When the wind does blow, don't furl the sail; when the fire does burn, don't pour cold water on it. What is more, though we cannot directly kindle the fire,

[1] *Maud*—Part I. Tennyson.

we can bring plenty of material for the burnt-offering to "the God who answers by fire" (I Kings 18 : 24). Praying the psalms, the hymns, the liturgy, reading and pondering the Scriptures, speaking to the Lord freely in extempore prayer, we too shall be able to say like the men of Emmaus "Did not our hearts burn within us while He talked to us on the road, while He opened to us the Scriptures?" (Luke 24 : 32). Whenever the heart is thus "strangely warmed", whenever we are "carried away", we can well afford to leave behind our plans or orders, and go wherever the Spirit leads.

PRAYING WITH THE WILL

We must love God with emotion, and yet the devotional life must not be based on emotion. The house of prayer must not be built on the shifting sand of feeling, but upon the immovable rock of the will. S. Luke describes how Jesus, as His ministry moved to the climax, "steadfastly set His face to go to Jerusalem". Let us borrow that expression to describe the true basis of the devotional life. The face must be set in the direction of God. There must be the will, the steadfast intention, the quiet determination to live in fellowship with God, and to give Him the glory due to His name. In practice, this means having a rule of prayer, however simple or modest. By keeping to it, we are delivered from the tyranny of mood and circumstance, and reserve in our busy lives a place for the worship of God. There should be a Quiet Time at the beginning and end of each day (see Chapter III), together with the habit of reading the Holy Scriptures (see Chapter IV). Such a rule should also include weekly habits of public worship, corporate prayer, and participation in the Holy Communion (see Chapter XII). Ideally, it should also include the habit of recollection, the practice of the presence of God throughout the day (see Chapter XIV). Each person must make his own rule of prayer, taking into account his own temperament, needs, and circumstances. This will to pray, this intention embodied in a rule, may be likened to the steel girders of a sky-scraper, or to the skeleton of an animal; out of sight—indeed, usually out of mind—it nevertheless gives cohesion and strength.

THE IMPORTANCE OF HABIT

It is hardly possible to exaggerate the importance of habit in prayer, as in life generally. The tendency to despise an activity because it is a habit is foolish and misguided. Good habits confer three benefits. By means of them we acquire or improve our abilities; many of our most valuable skills are due to the formation of habits. The mind also is set free to attend to other matters. Best of all, we are saved from the unnecessary strain of having to make decisions about everything. "Habit is the enormous flywheel of society, its most precious conservative agent. There is no more miserable human being than one in whom nothing is habitual but indecision. Full half the time of such a man goes to the deciding, or regretting, of matters which ought to be so ingrained in him as practically not to exist for his consciousness at all."[1] The habit of typing or of driving a car is useful, largely because the patterns of action no longer require the conscious attention of the mind, which is therefore set free for other activity. Going for a walk can be enjoyable because the mind is not preoccupied with the habit of walking. When prayer becomes habitual, the mind is set free in both the ways just mentioned. It is no longer necessary to keep on making decisions about place, time, method, and so on. Also in the act of prayer itself the mind, being no longer concerned with the "how", is free to attend to God. That is why a liturgy yields its full value only when it is thoroughly familiar through habit. When the attention of the worshipper is no longer preoccupied with the pattern of words and deeds, he is set free to worship God.

PRAYING WITH THE MIND

It has just been stated that the true function of habit in prayer is to set the mind free *to attend* to God. Habit is the servant of attention. It is abused, it becomes mere habit, mechanical repetition, when it is made a substitute for thought and understanding. That can easily happen. It is possible to say prayers, to sing psalms or hymns, to repeat the words of the

[1] *The Principles of Psychology*—William James.

liturgy, without any thought or attention at all. That is a wrong use of habit; but the abuse of a thing is no argument against its right use. Good habit is the servant of full attention. I can give creative thought to the composition of the letter I am typing, precisely because I need give so little attention to the technique of typing. "Habit and attention must therefore co-operate in the life of worship. Habit alone easily deteriorates into mechanical repetition, the besetting sin of the liturgical mind. Attention alone means, in the end, intolerable strain. Each partner has his weak point. Habit tends to routine—attention is apt to care for nothing but the experience of the moment, and ignore the need of a stable practice, independent of personal fluctuations. But it is the beautiful combination of order and spontaneity . . . which is the mark of a genuine spiritual maturity and indeed the fine flower of a worshipping life."[1] Attention should also be in working partnership with emotion as well as with habit. The apostle Paul did not belittle the place of emotion and ecstasy in the worship of the Church at Corinth, but he had no sympathy with any act of worship which left out intelligence and understanding. "If I pray in a tongue, my spirit prays but my mind is unfruitful. What am I to do? I will pray with the spirit, and I will pray with the mind also; I will sing with the spirit and I will sing with the mind also" (I Corinthians 14: 14, 15). Thought, reason, intelligence, understanding are to be fully engaged in praise, prayer, and utterance. Emotion without understanding becomes emotion-alism, and habit without understanding becomes formalism.

"I WILL PRAY WITH THE MIND"

"You shall love the Lord your God . . . with all your mind." There are several ways of obeying this part of the great com-mandment in our prayers.

I. When you sing a psalm or hymn, or say a written prayer, think of the meaning of what you are saying. Avoid the habit of saying a familiar prayer, such as the Lord's Prayer, without any attention to the meaning. Mean what you say. In extem-pore prayer, avoid the use of meaningless clichés and sentences. Say what you mean.

II. Give some thought to the content of your prayers before

[1] *Worship*—Evelyn Underhill (Nisbet).

praying. Look ahead over the coming day, or review the past day. Think a little before you make your confession or thanks-giving. Think of the needs of the other before you intercede, or of your own needs before offering petition. Think and pray.

III. Let meditation—that is to say, disciplined and sustained thinking about God—have a place, whenever possible, in your Quiet Time. Methods of doing this have already been considered in Chapter IV.

IV. Bring your full powers of intelligence to the study and practice of prayer. There are many Christians nowadays like Mundanus, who brought all his powers of reason and concentration to study methods of improving his business, but never gave a thought to prayer. "If Mundanus sees a book of devotion, he passes it by as he does a spelling book, because he remembers that he learned to pray so many years ago under his mother when he learned to spell."[1]

PRAYING WITH THE BODY

> Let us not always say
> "Spite of this flesh today,
> I strove, made head,
> Gained ground upon the whole.
> As the bird wings and sings,
> Let us cry 'All good things
> Are ours, nor soul helps flesh
> More than flesh helps soul'".

Because, as Robert Browning here says, the flesh may help the soul, the body also has a part in the prayer life. Man is not pure spirit, but embodied spirit; as Thomas a Kempis puts it "Thou art man, and not God, thou art flesh and no angel". It is therefore unwise to leave the body out of account in offering our prayers. To say that our actions are the expression of our thoughts and emotions is only one-half of the truth. The expressive actions of the body can also quicken and strengthen thought and emotion. What happens when I see a bull in the field where I am walking? Do I run away because I am afraid, or am I afraid because I run away? The psychologists James and Lange hav: emphassied the truth in the second

[1] *A Serious Call to a Devout and Holy Life*—William Law.

part of that question. Emotion may lead to action, but action also evokes and strengthens emotion. I feel more angry when I clench my fists and strike a blow. If I make myself smile and burst into laughter, I shall probably begin to feel cheerful. The expressive action of the body does react for good or ill on the human spirit. Love to God or man grows by means of the acts which express it. It was the denial of this truth which led Baron von Hügel to say "What a curious psychology which allows me to kiss my child because I love it, but strictly forbids me to kiss it in order to love it".[1] This principle has an important bearing on the devotional life.

SOME EXPRESSIVE ACTIONS

The people of the Bible were not afraid to pray with their bodies. "O come, let us worship and *bow down*, let us kneel before the Lord our Maker!" (Psalm 95: 6). Jesus looked up to heaven, or knelt upon the earth when He prayed (John 17: 1; Luke 22: 41). The primitive Christians prayed "lifting holy hands" (I Timothy 2: 8). It is a good thing to practise praying in any position, standing, sitting, lying, kneeling, for there may be times, such as a prolonged illness, when kneeling is not possible. But the act of kneeling can be a fine expression of submission and reverence to God. Christians have also found it helpful to fold the hands for prayer, like the Roman soldier placing his hands between those of the commander as he made his oath of allegiance. Let us use our lips to *say* our prayers, for that is more helpful than just thinking them in the mind. Prayer is conversation, and thought should be expressed in word. We cannot always say our prayers out loud, because of the presence or proximity of others; but it is usually possible. To stand, to kneel, to bow, to prostrate oneself, to lift up the hands, to close the eyes, to cover the face, to fold the hands, to speak, to sing, to kiss the Holy Scriptures—these are some of the ways in which worship can be expressed through the body. In saying this, we have been using the word "body", as is now customary, of the flesh, the physical frame and organism. But in the Bible, the word has a much richer connotation. It stands for the whole personality, the total man. All that is written in this chapter is therefore summed up in Paul's great

[1] *Selected Letters*—Friedrich von Hügel.

appeal, "Present your bodies as a living sacrifice, holy and acceptable to God, which is your spiritual worship" (Romans 12: 1).

SUMMARY

I. The whole personality of man should be involved and expressed in the worship of God.

II. Feeling is a part, not the whole of prayer; it is a mistake to pray only when you feel like it.

III. We can master our moods by making prayer a matter of rule or habit.

IV. Emotion gives warmth, richness and depth to the prayer life.

V. Do not stifle, but gladly accept spontaneous emotion.

VI. The devotional life must be based upon the will; upon a rule of prayer.

VII. Habit stabilises prayer and sets the mind free to attend to God.

VIII. Without thought and understanding, habit degenerates into mere routine, emotion into emotionalism.

IX. There are four ways of praying fully with the mind. Think of the meaning of what you are saying; think about your prayers before you pray; let meditation have a place in the Quiet Time; study the practice of prayer.

X. The expressive actions of the body can quicken and strengthen the inner life of devotion.

CHAPTER TWELVE

PRAYING WITH THE CHURCH

CHRIST PRAYED WITH OTHERS

"But when you pray, go into your room and shut the door and pray to your Father who is in secret" (Matthew 6: 6). So far in this book we have been thinking of the individual praying alone in the secret place. Christ taught us to do this, and He did it Himself. Early in the morning, late in the evening, He withdrew to the solitary place, the hill-side, the garden, for personal communion with God. But this is only one aspect of His prayer life. He who prayed alone, also prayed with others. It was His custom to share in the public worship of the synagogue, in the praises and prayers, in the public reading and exposition of the Scriptures. Even His withdrawals were not necessarily for solitary prayer. "Now it happened that as He was praying alone the disciples were with Him" (Luke 9: 18). When He went up into a high mountain to pray, He took with Him Peter, James and John (Luke 9: 28). These same three intimate friends also accompanied Him into the Garden of Gethsemane, and they must have overheard His prayer, otherwise it could not have been recorded (Mark 14: 33). In the Upper Room, Christ, on behalf of the whole company, gave thanks over the loaf and the cup (Mark 14: 22, 23). On that same night when He was betrayed, "He lifted up His eyes to heaven", and in the presence of the apostles, prayed for them and for the whole Church of the future (John 17). Cavalry was no solitary place; yet Jesus prayed there (Luke 23: 34 and 46). Immediately after the resurrection the disciples were meeting for corporate prayer. It was upon a company at prayer that the Holy Spirit was poured out on the Day of Pentecost (The Acts 1: 14). The first converts "devoted themselves to the apostles' teaching and fellowship, to the breaking of bread and the prayers" (The Acts 2: 42). The Lord had prayed habitually with the apostles, and from the very beginning the apostolic Church was a community at prayer. If we are to "follow in His steps", we must pray alone and we must pray with others.

THE ADVANTAGES OF PRAYING TOGETHER

What are the advantages, the fruits, the blessings of praying together? The greatest is the covenanted *presence* of Christ. The promise of His real presence is given in close association with a saying about prayer. "Again I say to you, if two of you agree on earth about anything they ask, it will be done for them by my Father in heaven. For where two or three are gathered in my name, there am I in the midst of them" (Matthew 18: 19, 20). The Jewish rabbis used to say that when two people met to study the Law, the Shekinah, the Presence, was between them. All down the ages, Christians assembled with one accord for prayer, have been aware of the unseen presence, have encountered the living Lord. Corporate prayer also *quickens and kindles* the spirit of the individual as he shares in the common life and action. The experience of Martin Luther is typical. "At home, in my own house, there is no warmth or vigour in me, but in the church when the multitude is gathered together, a fire is kindled in my heart and it breaks its way through." The coals in the fire glow and burn brightly together; take one coal out of the fire, place it separately on the hearth, and it is soon extinguished. This does not mean that the devotion of an individual languishes because it is private. It may grow cold because it is not *also* corporate. Both are necessary. We "maintain the spiritual glow" in our private prayers by praying with others, in our corporate prayers by praying privately. There is also *a deeper joy* in praying together, an added vitality, a plus difficult to define. It is rather like the difference between eating your supper alone, and sharing in a party feast. It is not just a matter of food, nor would one always desire the latter in preference to the former. Eating together is not the same as eating in solitude; the something more is the company, the fellowship. So it is with prayer. Lastly, praying together is the best way of *learning* how to pray. Prayer is conversation, and we converse in company. Whoever learned to talk in solitude? We learn best to converse with God in the company of those who pray to Him.

Now a prayer circle may be small or large. The number

praying together may vary from a minimum of two to a maximum of several hundreds. Here we shall consider four circles of prayer, proceeding from the smallest to the largest. There is the tiny cell of two or three, the larger prayer group or meeting, the local Church and the universal Church.

"WHERE TWO OR THREE ARE GATHERED"

As Cleopas and his friend walked to Emmaus on the first Easter Day, the Risen Lord joined them and talked to them on the way. This can happen always, when two or three believers commune together. When two Christians really meet, that is, enter into deep fellowship, they always meet the third. Should there not be, at an appropriate time, some recognition of this? Should not the two, like Cleopas and his friend (his wife?), cease conversing with each other in order to converse with the Lord? The two may be husband and wife, praying together in the home at the beginning or the end of the day, or on some special occasion of thankfulness or need. The two or three may be father, mother and children, praying as a family after breakfast, or at the bedside of the children at night. The two may be close friends who, having spent a pleasant evening chatting by the fire, conclude by talking to God. The two or three may be Christians who, having a common concern to win others for Christ, meet to intercede. Such tiny prayer cells have great value. The private devotion of each individual is quickened and enriched. Because the two or three "agree", are in deep personal concord, have a unity of purpose, their prayers are answered (Matthew 18: 19). Mutual confidence makes it possible to pray with a fullness and intimacy not possible even in a prayer meeting. Best of all, the fellowship between the members of the cell is strengthened and fulfilled, as together they enter into communion with the Lord.

THE PRAYER GROUP

In addition to formal corporate worship, the service of the Word and the celebration of the Eucharist, Christians from the beginning met for prayer. After the Ascension and before Pentecost, the Apostles with the Holy Family "devoted themselves to prayer" (The Acts 1: 14). In the crisis of persecution, the assembled Church spontaneously resorted to prayer (The Acts 4: 23–31). When Peter was imprisoned and threatened with execution "many were gathered together and were praying" (The Acts 12: 12). As regards numbers, the prayer meeting is usually about midway between the tiny cell and the local Church. But this is not the main way in which it differs from both. The dominant purpose of a prayer meeting is intercession. The Christians had assembled in "the house of Mary, the mother of John whose other name was Mark" to pray for the release of Peter. There was a single aim—intercession. A prayer group meets to co-operate through prayer with the purpose of God in the lives of others. This is a work, a ministry, making demands on the time, the interest, and the energies of those sharing in it. The members of a prayer group may be engaged in a common task—they may be teachers in a school, nurses in a hospital, workers in a youth organisation. Sharing a common concern, they meet to intercede for those with whom they work. When this is not the case, as in a Church prayer meeting, the purpose of the gathering, the topics for intercession, the prayer objectives, must be set clearly before the people. Such definiteness is the life of a prayer meeting. There must be something as definite and urgent as the release of Peter from prison. There always is. It requires imagination and leadership to define it and to convey the sense of urgency. Perhaps the best kind of prayer group is that which combines study and action with intercession. Here, the study of the Bible strengthens the faith and fellowship of those who pray for others, and go forth to act upon their prayers.

THE PURPOSE AND PATTERN OF WORSHIP

We come now to the best known and most important way in which Christians pray together—the corporate worship of the local Church. What takes place in a Church service? All that was said in Chapter I about the chief purposes of prayer is directly applicable here. The main purpose of corporate worship, as of private prayer, is fellowship with God. This fellowship has two aspects, giving and receiving. This two fold movement, this rhythm of offering and taking, underlies all that we do in worship and is the key to its meaning. The patriarch Jacob in a vision, saw a stone stairway reaching up from earth to heaven. On this "ladder" there was a two-way traffic. The messengers of God were ascending from Jacob to God, and descending from God to Jacob. We may take this as an illustration of what goes on in true worship. Like the ascending angels, our praises and prayers, our gifts and the oblation of our lives, go up to God and are accepted by Him. This is the approach of man to God, worship as offering. But this movement is itself a response to the descending God, who comes to His worshippers, addresses them in scripture and preaching, and gives Himself in word and sacrament. The purpose of this two-fold movement is encounter, meeting, communion. We come to church to meet the Lord, to receive the Lord, to give ourselves to the Lord.

HOW TO TAKE PART IN A SERVICE

Since worship is the most important thing we ever do, man's chief end, we ought to do it as well as we can. That means doing four things.

I. Prepare yourself thoroughly for worship. As already suggested, this preparation should begin at home. Devote the Saturday evening prayer-time to an act of self-examination and confession. Receive God's forgiveness, so that you come to worship on the Lord's Day "with a clean mind and a pure heart". The Sunday morning Quiet Time may include intercession for the ministry and the services of the day. This preparation should be continued in the church building. Be present at least five minutes before the service begins. Spend a few moments in prayer, asking the help of the Holy Spirit for all those leading the service, for your fellow-worshippers and for yourself. Those few moments of quiet are invaluable. Don't try to pack too much into them; relax, quieten the mind, recollect the presence of God.

II. Participate fully in the worship. A church is not a theatre; you have not come to be a spectator of something done by others. You are yourself a part of the drama. Participate in the common action, the concerted movement of the whole worshipping congregation—"that *together* you may with *one* voice glorify the God and Father of our Lord Jesus Christ" (Romans 15: 6). Join wholeheartedly in the worship, with all those who are present. Sing the psalms, canticles, hymns. Join fully in the liturgy, the responses, the Amens. Don't hum and mumble—sing and say! Let the whole of you, your understanding, your emotions, your will, your body, participate. What you receive from worship depends upon what you put into it.

III. Listen intently to God in worship. You have come to meet with God and to hear what He has to say to you. He will speak through the reading of the scriptures and the preaching of the word. Don't come to hear a human being, or to pass judgement upon what you hear. Come to hear the Lord God, that you may obey His word. Of course we have to sift the wheat from the chaff—and sometimes there is a lot of chaff! But keep the main purpose always in mind. "Speak, Lord, for Thy servant hears."

IV. Offer yourself to God in the worship. You have come to give; worship is offering. "Like living stones be yourselves built into a spiritual house, to be a holy priesthood, to *offer* spiritual sacrifices acceptable to God through Jesus Christ" (I Peter 2: 5). Sing the psalms, hymns, canticles, anthems *to God*, as a sacrifice of praise. Offer up the prayers *to God*. Share fully in the Offertory. This is not just the offering of money, but that of which money is the token—our daily work. Like Cain and Abel in the Bible, we offer the products of our toil, that all our work may be dedicated to God. These spiritual sacrifices of praise, prayer and gift, can only be acceptable, if they are all alike tokens of the oblation of oneself. You have not worshipped unless you have offered yourself to God. "I appeal to you therefore, brethren, by the mercies of God, to present your bodies as a living sacrifice, holy and acceptable to God, which is your spiritual worship" (Romans 12: 1).

THE HOLY COMMUNION

In the service variously called the Breaking of Bread, the Lord's Supper, the Holy Communion, the Eucharist, the prayers of the individual and of the Church reach a climax. Instituted by the Lord Himself, this primitive Christian service, the pattern of all worship, can be the centre and inspiration of all our devotion. Writing to the Philippians, St. Paul gives a twofold description of the worship of the New Covenant. "For we are the true circumcision, who worship by the Spirit of God, and glory in Christ Jesus" (3: 3). This glorying in Christ Jesus, incarnate, crucified, risen, exalted, in the power of the Holy Spirit is the supreme purpose of the Eucharist. This Christocentric service, which is both personal and corporate, something said and something done, can transform all our devotion into a glorying in Christ Jesus. We come to the Lord's Table in order to do five things.

I. Give Thanks. The Lord's Supper was called the Eucharist by the Fathers of the Early Church; this is the Greek word for Thanksgiving. In accordance with Jewish custom, at the Last Supper the Lord Jesus gave thanks over the loaf and the cup, thereby consecrating them to God. We give thanks for the body and the blood of Christ. By the sacrifice and victory of the cross and the resurrection, we have been redeemed from sin and death. We are grateful to Christ for what He has done and continues to be. The Eucharist is a feast, a festival of gladness, a service of triumph. In every part of the rite, but especially in the great prayer of thanksgiving which consecrates, we express our gratitude to God for Christ crucified, risen and present. Come to give thanks.

II. Remember. When the Lord Jesus gave thanks over the loaf He said, "This is my body which is for you. Do this in remembrance of me." After giving thanks over the cup He said, "This cup is the new covenant in my blood. Do this, as often as you drink it, in *remembrance* of me" (I Corinthians II: 24, 25). The English word "remembrance" translates the Greek word "anamnesis" which in Latin was rendered "memoria". But when we speak of the Lord's Supper as a memorial, we must take care to recover the biblical meaning of the word "remembrance". Nowadays, to remember is to recall a past event or an absent person. But in the Lord's Supper, Christ is not absent but present, and His sacrifice is not only a past event, but also a continuing reality. In our worship we enter the holy place, we join Christ our High Priest in heaven, where He offers Himself perpetually to the Father. Christ and His sacrifice is present, and is re-called, set forth, re-presented in the Eucharist. This is the meaning of "anamnesis". The past event, the sacrifice of the cross, is made operative in the present, as we join Christ at the heavenly altar. Come to recall.

III. Take. "The cup of blessing which we bless, is it not a *participation* in the blood of Christ? The bread which we break, is it not a *participation* in the body of Christ?" (I Corinthians 10: 16). Here the word translated "participation" (Koinonia) is variously rendered as fellowship, communion, sharing, partnership. "Holy Communion" means joint-participation in the body and blood of Christ. "Body" in the Bible means "personality"—the whole person; and "blood" is life which has been sacrificed. In the Lord's Supper, we are joint-participators in the personality of the risen Christ, in the life which has passed through death. We do not come to receive *something*, a substance; we come to receive a Person, who is mediated through the word and the fellowship, the actions and the elements. Come to receive Him.

IV. Vow. In the Roman Empire, the word "sacrament" was used of the pledge or vow of allegiance made by the soldier, as he placed his folded hands between those of the Commander. Our vow of loyalty to Christ made in the sacrament of Baptism is constantly renewed in the sacrament of the Holy Table. This is a pledge not only of loyalty to Christ, but also to all those who share with us in His sacrificed life. We undertake to live in covenanted or bonded love with the members of His Body. The holy kiss of love and peace, "the sacrament of friendship", which was part of the primitive rite, is a symbol of this. Come to pledge your loyalty to Christ and the Church.

V. Offer. The Eucharist is a sacrifice. We offer our praises and our prayers, the gifts of bread and wine, the eucharistic prayer which is a sacrifice of praise and thanksgiving, together with the oblation of our own lives "to be a reasonable, holy and living sacrifice". All this we do in union with Christ, whose sacrifice we show forth and re-present, and in whom we offer ourselves to the Father. Come to offer yourself with Christ.

THE UNIVERSAL CHURCH

The individual, the cell, the group, the local Church at prayer, are all part of the universal Church, "which is the blessed company of all faithful people". It is never possible for us to meet and pray with the whole Church; even the largest and most representative gathering of Christians is but a tiny part of it. Yet, in fact, it is never possible for Christians to meet and pray apart from the whole Church. My whole body acts when I turn over a page with my little finger. The devotion of the individual, the prayers of the two or three gathered in Christ's name, the worship of the local Church, each Eucharist—these are actions of the whole Body of Christ. It is important to pray consciously and deliberately with the whole Church. It helps to remember that the Bible you read, the psalms, hymns, canticles you sing or repeat, the prayers of the liturgy you say, are being used by Christians all over the world. Remember that when you begin to pray, you are joining in an activity which is already going on apart from you, and which will continue when you have ceased your devotions.

> "The sun that bids us rest is waking
> our brethren 'neath the western sky
> and hour by hour fresh lips are making
> Thy wondrous doings heard on high."

It can be a great joy and satisfaction to add your own small quota to the unceasing worship of the one, holy, catholic and apostolic Church. And that does not only mean "the holy Church throughout all the world". At worship the Church militant is one with the Church triumphant. We praise God with the glorious company of the apostles, the goodly fellowship of the prophets, the noble army of martyrs, with a great multitude which no man can number, with angels and archangels and all the company of heaven. When you are face to face with the Father, you are with the whole family.

SUMMARY

I. Christ our example, prayed with others as well as in solitude.

II. The blessings of corporate prayer are—the assurance of Christ's presence, the quickening and kindling of devotion, a deeper joy through sharing, education in praying.

III. Christian partners and friends, should seize every opportunity of praying together.

IV. A prayer-group co-operates with God through intercession; it should have definite objectives and a sense of urgency.

V. Christian worship is a two-way fellowship with God in which He speaks and gives Himself to us in word and sacrament, and we give ourselves to Him in praise, prayer, offertory and oblation.

VI. Putting the best into a service means—careful preparation, whole-hearted participation, attentive listening, complete self-offering.

VII. We do five things at the Lord's Supper—give thanks for Christ, remember Christ, receive Christ, vow allegiance to Christ, offer ourselves with Christ.

VIII. We should offer our prayers as part of the unceasing worship of the whole Church militant and triumphant.

CHAPTER THIRTEEN

PRAYING FROM BOOKS

TWO WAYS OF PRAYING

THERE are two main ways of praying. The first of these is usually called extempore prayer. This is making up or composing our own prayers as we go along. In normal conversation, we do not prepare what we are going to say in advance. We speak our thoughts freely as they enter the mind. Not necessarily without deliberation, for we know the wisdom of the advice "think before you speak". In prayer there may well be a good deal of deliberation before speaking. Isaac Watts distinguishes between *free prayer* "done by some work of meditation before we begin to speak in prayer" and *extempore prayer* "when we without any reflection or meditation beforehand address ourselves to God and speak the thoughts of our hearts as fast as we conceive them". But this kind of prayer, whether free or extempore, whether spoken after or without deliberation, is the product or composition of the individual offering it. The second main way of praying is the use of the prepared, written prayers of others. These may be taken from the psalter or the hymnal, from the liturgy or from books of prayer. Sometimes these two ways of praying are set in violent antithesis, as if one way were altogether right and the other altogether wrong. The preference is largely a matter of ecclesiastical tradition. Those accustomed to the use of liturgical prayer in public, often use written prayers in private. Those accustomed to free prayer in public worship, tend to use extempore prayer only in private. But why choose between them? The devil's pastime is the creation of false antitheses— and this is one of them. It is not a case of "either—or", but of "both—and".

THE VALUE OF EXTEMPORE AND OF WRITTEN PRAYER

When it is remembered that prayer is conversation with God, the value of free or extempore prayer is obvious. In the directness of a personal meeting and relationship, we are accustomed to speak on impulse, with spontaneity. We "speak the thoughts of our hearts as fast as we conceive them". The conversation arises out of the immediate situation and has relevance to it. So with extempore prayer. It has all the values of directness and intimacy, is relevant to the situation, related to the unique circumstances. On the other hand there are values just as great in written prayer and liturgical worship. Here beauty of language and thought is combined with order and dignity. Written prayer also has great educational value. In using it, we are inviting the wise, the mature, those who have walked closely with God, to teach us how to pray. We are saved from narrowness of interest, taken beyond our own immediate concerns, encouraged to widen the area of our prayers. We are led to pray about many things which would not otherwise have concerned us. Written prayers are also of great value in times of special difficulty, spiritual dryness, bodily weakness or illness, weariness, or distress. We can rely upon the help of others, when the creative effort of making our own prayers is well-nigh impossible. Their function at other times is like that of the self-starter in a car, which is no longer used when the engine has started up. A written prayer can quicken the spirit of devotion, and prepare the way for extempore prayer. Much more important, by the use of common prayer, the devotion of the individual is linked to that of the local and the universal Church. And not only with the Church of today, but with the Church of past ages, which is now the Church triumphant. It is one way of praying with others, even when alone. Where are we to find these written prayers for the enrichment of private devotion? We now consider the four main sources.

THE PSALTER

The Book of Psalms is the original praise- and prayer-book of Temple, Synagogue, and Church. Its influence on both private devotion and corporate worship has been greater than that of any other book. While the dominant note is that of praise, all the chief kinds of prayer are represented. There are psalms of adoration (Psalm 145), thanksgiving, (103), penitence (51), petition (61), intercession (80), meditation (139), affirmation of faith (23). Four main strands are to be found in the Psalter—nature, the history of the people of God, the worship of the temple, the experience and piety of the individual. This gives to the collection a rich variety and catholicity of outlook. The combination of the personal and the corporate, the "I" and the "we", enables the individual to praise and pray with the Church, which is one of the characteristics of a mature devotional life. There are several ways of using the Psalter in private prayer. We should of course read and meditate on the psalms, in order to understand them and receive their message. But in addition to this they should be read aloud, prayed to God. One way is to pray one psalm each day at the beginning of the Quiet Time, going through the whole book in sequence. Not all the psalms, however, are equally suitable for private prayer, and the individual is well advised to make his own selection. This can be done by buying a separate copy of the Psalter, and marking or underlining all the parts chosen for devotional use. Alternatively, selected psalms may be copied into one's own prayer-book.[1] The regular use of even a small number of great psalms can effect the whole quality of devotion. Take trouble to memorise a few, and you will be amply rewarded.

THE HYMNAL

The early Christians not only used the ancient psalms, they also composed "psalms and hymns and spiritual songs" of their own (Colossians 3: 16). Fragments of these hymns are preserved in the New Testament itself (e.g. Ephesians 5: 14 and I Timothy 2: 16). Today, the hymnal of any of the historic Churches includes great hymns of all the centuries and traditions. This is a precious part of our devotional heritage, and each individual should possess his own copy of the hymnal for constant use along with the Bible and the Psalter. Some hymns are acts of joyful praise, songs of adoration, others are prayers of thanksgiving, penitence, petition, intercession, dedication, addressed directly to the Father, to the Son, to the Holy Spirit,

[1] I have selected seventy psalms especially suitable for devotion, together with other ancient canticles and prayers, in *Responsive Praises and Prayers for Minister and Congregation*—Hodder & Stoughton, 2s 6d.

or to the Holy Trinity. Yet others are confessions of faith. Hymns, unless they are being used for meditation, should be said or sung to God. How should the hymns used in a Quiet Time be selected? The hymnal has a pattern, the hymns are arranged according to subject. It is often helpful to follow the sequence of the Christian Year, selecting the hymns appropriate to Advent, Christmas, Epiphany, Lent, Passiontide, Easter, Ascension, Whitsun or Trinity. There are also special seasons or occasions in life when certain hymns are appropriate—morning, evening, spring, harvest, baptism, communion, marriage, bereavement. Hymns may also be related to the current series of Bible readings, e.g. the Gospels with hymns on the Ministry of Christ, the Epistle to the Hebrews with hymns on the Priesthood of Christ, the Book of Revelation with hymns on the Life Everlasting. The desires to express something, penitence or thankfulness; the need of something, encouragement or inspiration; and sometimes just inclination, may rightly determine the choice of a hymn.

THE LITURGY

The word "liturgy" (leitourgia) taken from the New Testament, is used of *service* rendered either to God or man. The priestly service of Zechariah, the father of John the Baptist, in the Temple at Jerusalem, is described as his liturgy (Luke 1: 23). The contribution of a sum of money by the Gentile Churches for the relief of the poor at Jerusalem is also described as a liturgy. The whole life and activity of the true Christian, whether in church or in the world is liturgy, Divine Service. Here we are concerned with liturgy as worship. If our corporate worship is to give full expression to the gospel, it must have a certain pattern and content. This pattern of words and actions, the gospel embodied in worship, is the liturgy. It has two main parts. There is "the liturgy of the word", the reading and exposition of Scriptures with praises and prayers, and "the liturgy of the Upper Room", the Holy Communion. In addition to the Scriptures, we have already considered part of this liturgy; the psalms and the hymns. But the prayers also, used at the service of the Word and the Eucharist, may be used for the enrichment of private devotion. This is especially true of the ancient praises and prayers of the undivided Church.

Of these mention may be made of the great scriptural canticles: the Magnificat (Luke 1: 46–55), the Benedictus (Luke 1: 68–74), and the Nunc Dimittis (Luke 2: 29–32), so often sung at the service of the Word. The frequent use of these keeps the mind centred on the great acts of our redemption in Christ. The Te Deum ("We praise Thee, O God"), is a magnificent act of praise, and a full confession of faith. Using the most ancient parts of the Communion Service, the Sursum Corda ("Lift up your hearts") down to the Sanctus ("Holy, holy, holy"), and the Gloria in Excelsis ("Glory be to God on high"), we can join in adoration, thanksgiving, and supplication with the Church of all ages. The ancient collects used at the Eucharist are also of great value in private prayer. As the word implies, these strong, concise prayers were used to collect, to sum up all the silent prayers of the congregation. Some seventy of these collects from the old Latin Sacramentaries were translated by Cranmer for the Anglican Book of Common Prayer.[1] In using them in the first person plural, the Christian can pray for the Church, local and universal, and for his friends and neighbours as well as for himself.

MAKING YOUR OWN PRAYER-BOOK

The orders, or the books of prayer compiled or composed by others, can also be of help in the devotional life. The use of one such book for a limited time can introduce freshness and variety into devotion, and enlarge sympathy and understanding. In *Prayers and Praises*, Dr. Nathaniel Micklem, making full use of the ancient canticles and collects, of psalms, hymns, and well-known prayers, has compiled offices for the mornings and the evenings of one week.[2] *A Diary of Private Prayer* by Dr. John Baillie provides morning and evening prayers for one month. Here the daily prayers are shorter and more personal, and opposite each order is a blank page for notes, names, or prayers.[3] *Great Souls at Prayer*, compiled by Mrs. Mary W. Tileston, "fourteen centuries of prayer, praise, and aspiration,

[1] Many of these ancient collects are to be found in *Great Souls at Prayer*—Mary W. Tileston (Allenson & Co.). The collects of the *Book of Common Prayer* will be found in *Daily Prayer*—E. Milner-White and G. W. Briggs (Oxford University Press, pp. 123–144).

[2] Hodder & Stoughton.   [3] Oxford University Press.

from S. Augustine to Christina Rossetti and Robert Louis Stevenson", contains many of the ancient collects, and has one or two prayers for every day of one year.[1] All three books are excellent. But as well as using the books of others, why not make your own prayer-book? After all, each person is unique, and can best express his own devotion in writing. Buy a good, well-bound, lined book. Copy into it whatever is likely to be of value to you in your devotional life. It may contain your patterns, bare outlines without any written prayers for your morning and evening Quiet Times (see Chapter VI). Copy into it your weekly plan(s) of Thanksgiving or of Intercession; and the lists of individuals for whom you intend to pray regularly. Compile your own full orders for morning and evening prayer, assigning a place for Bible reading and extempore prayer. Some of these prayers you can compose yourself. They may have no literary value, but that does not matter. If you think out and write down carefully a thanksgiving, a confession, a petition, an intercession, a dedication, it may be of great value to you, when you use the order later on. Copy into your orders some of the psalms and hymns, the canticles and collects, the great prayers of the liturgy or of devout individuals. In this connection, two books will be of great help—*A Chain of Prayer Across the Ages*[2] and *Daily Prayer*.[3] Many of the great prayers will be found in one or other of these books. A good personal prayer-book can weave together three strands which should all be present in the devotional life. The written prayers of others, our own written prayers, and extempore prayer make a three-fold cord which is not easily broken.

SUMMARY

I. There are two main ways of praying, each of which has value.

II. Extempore Prayer is direct, intimate, flexible, and relevant.

III. Written prayer has beauty and dignity, educates the mind, is of special value in times of dryness and weakness; it

[1] Allenson & Co., Ltd.

[2] Compiled by Selina Fitzherbert Fox (John Murray).

[3] By E. Milner-White and G. W. Briggs (Oxford University Press).

can kindle the spirit of devotion and link the praying individual with the Church.

IV. The Psalter, the original praise- and prayer-book, a combination of the personal and corporate, is of incomparable value in the devotional life.

V. A Quiet Time can be enriched by the use of hymns, appropriate to the season or special occasion.

VI. The great prayers of the liturgy, especially the canticles and collects, can also enrich private devotion, and enable the individual to pray with the Church.

VII. Compile your own prayer-book, combining the written prayers of others and your own written prayers, with extempore prayer.

CHAPTER FOURTEEN

THE PRACTICE OF THE PRESENCE OF GOD

"DEVOTION is neither private nor public prayer; but prayers, whether private or public, are particular parts or instances of devotion. Devotion signifies a life given, or devoted, to God." So far in this book we have been thinking about what William Law here calls "prayers, whether private or public". Our concern has been with the daily Quiet Time, the special period or periods set apart in the morning or in the evening for communion with God. In Chapter XII attention was given to those occasions when we meet to pray or worship with others. But throughout we have been preoccupied with *special times* of prayer, private or public, and with what should be done in them. In the opening sentence, just quoted, of that great devotional classic "A Serious Call to a Devout and Holy Life", William Law warns us against mistaking the part for the whole. Private and public prayers are necessary—but they are only "parts or instances". Devotion must include the whole of life; it *is* life devoted to God. In these last three chapters, we shall be concerned with this truth and its far-reaching implications.

WALKING WITH GOD

At the beginning of Chapter III, the question was raised "Are prayer-times necessary?" Reference was then made to an important principle, the implications of which were not developed at that point. It is by the consecration of one special part, that we are enabled to consecrate the whole. We keep the Lord's Day holy, so that all days may be sacred; the Lord's Table holy, so that all our meals may be sacraments; the Lord's House holy, so that all creation may be His temple. The special times of prayer, therefore, whether in the quiet room or in the church, are not to be regarded as ends in themselves. They are not intended to be little islands of fellowship and peace, cut off from the great continent of ordinary life.

Rather, they are to be observed in order that the whole of life may be fellowship with God. This truth is finely expressed in the metaphor of "walking with God", which is found in many parts of the Bible. Two people walking together have the same destination, and the joy of companionship on the way towards it. They converse often together; and it is a two-way conversation of listening and speaking. At times they neither speak nor listen, but walk along together in silent thought, yet each fully aware of the presence of the other. So is communion with God. We have our regular times of private and public prayer, when we speak to Him, and read and listen to His word. But these special times are only *part* of our communion. We are to be with Him even when we are not speaking or listening to Him. How can the Christian continue to walk with God, when he leaves the secret chamber or the chapel?

TAKING OUR PRAYING INTO OUR LIVING

One thing we should do, is to take praying out into living. It is a mistake to confine prayer to the sacred times and places, the quiet room, the prayer-group, the church. We must, of course, retire to pray, but it is no less important to pray in the actual setting of life's demands and events. Eliezer, the servant of Abraham, was praying as he stood by the well, with the camels kneeling, and the maidens approaching to draw water (Genesis 24: 12–14). Nehemiah did not consider it necessary to retire to his room to pray for guidance: there was no time for that. As he stood in the dining hall, offering the cup to the Persian Emperor, he prayed to the God of heaven (Nehemiah 2: 4). The Saviour, who habitually sought the solitary place, also prayed as they were nailing His hands to the cross, in the presence of the soldiers and with the crowds standing around (Luke 23: 24). Paul gave thanks for his daily food on the deck of a storm-tossed ship, in the presence of the passengers and crew (The Acts 27: 35). These are but a few examples, taken from the Bible, of concise prayers offered up *in the setting of events*, by men who walked with God. Usually, as in the case of Eliezer and Nehemiah, no one need know that prayer is being offered; it often is, and sometimes is not desirable to conceal it. Why conceal the fact that you are "saying grace", just because you are eating in a public restaurant? But whether secretly or not, let us pray in life-situations, in the setting of events, so that praying and living may be one, woven together like the warp and woof of a garment.

EJACULATORY PRAYER

Ejaculatory, derived from the Greek word for a javelin, is used to describe those short, pointed, sentence-prayers of deep desire, which are thrown out to God in the setting of common life. The swift upward look of adoration and trust, when there is time for nothing more; the loving repetition of the sacred name of Jesus; the lifting up of the heart in a word of gratitude—such fleeting acts help to keep us in unbroken communion with God. The housewife washing up at the sink sings the verse of a familiar hymn of praise, as acceptable to God in the kitchen as in church. The sick visitor crossing the hospital quadrangle offers up a prayer of intercession for the patient about to be seen. The worker waiting in the ante-room for an important interview, sends up to God an "arrow prayer" for strength and guidance. The old man sitting in his armchair by the fire confesses there and then the malicious thought he has been harbouring in his mind, and asks for God's forgiveness. The father, reading an encouraging letter from his son, responds with a prayer of thanksgiving to God. All these, in the setting of ordinary life and common events, have established the habit of ejaculatory prayer. For in this case the prayer is only a word, a phrase, a sentence. It is like a telegram, conveying a significant message in a minimum of words, but those few words winged with strong desire are a communication with God.

THINKING ABOUT GOD

Communion with God, however, is not just a matter of words, few or many. Two friends walking together are not necessarily talking all the time. We can be aware of God's presence even where there is no message to communicate, no prayer to be uttered. Of course a Christian cannot always be thinking of his Lord. No human father would be so unreasonable as to require that his son should always be thinking about him! During most of the day, our thoughts are rightly concentrated upon people, events, and the tasks with which we are occupied. Dr. William Temple once said that a man driving a bus down Oxford Street, London, during "the rush hour", ought not to be thinking about God. He is pleased when we attend to our work, or to the people around us, through both of which we are also dealing with Him. We are not, then, required to think about God all the time, or even (on ordinary days) most of the time. On the other hand, when one person loves another, the recollection of the absent loved one takes place many times during the course of the day. "For where your treasure is, there will your heart be also" (Matthew 6: 21). Our thoughts wander readily in the direction of those we dearly love. So much so, that we can say with pardonable exaggeration, "You are always in my thoughts." If we love the Lord, who is not absent, though invisible, the thought of Him and of His nearness will come frequently to mind. Of course, no one of us loves the Lord as he ought. That is why it is helpful to establish the habit of turning our thoughts to God during the odd moments of the day. For love grows by means of the acts which express it. As Brother Lawrence puts it, "We must know before we can love. In order to know God, we must often think of Him; and when we come to love Him, we shall then also think of Him often, for our heart will be with our treasure."

AIDS TO RECOLLECTION

"We must often think of Him." There are many practical ways of learning how to do this. One man stuck a bit of stamp-paper on the glass of his watch, to remind him of the presence of God. Many times during the course of the day he would glance at his watch—to see if it were time to get up, time for morning coffee, time for that afternoon engagement. In all these circumstances that piece of stamp-paper would say "You are here and now in the presence of God". Another person associates a certain street, along which he passes twice daily to and from the railway station, with the presence of God. A farmer recollects the presence whenever he opens any of the gates on his farm. Times, places, objects, events, people, may all be associated in the mind with the thought of God's

presence; and may thus be used to lead us to God, instead of
taking us away from God. The Hebrews were commanded by
God to wear tassels on their garments, to remind them of His
commandments (Numbers 15: 37–40). Of course tassels have
nothing to do with commandments. The association is entirely
arbitrary. Any other thing, carried about and seen constantly,
would have served equally as well. It was a useful device, a
practical aid to remembrance. We too are forgetful creatures;
we too need aids to recollection. With a little imagination,
each person can make his own.

USE THE ODD MOMENTS

If we are to practise the presence of God in these ways, then
we must learn to make good and fruitful use of the odd moments of the day. For every day has its odd moments when
the mind is free from necessary preoccupations. There are the
times we spend cooling our heels on railway platforms, standing in queues or waiting at the barber's. What use do we make
of the time spent on bus or train journeys, or standing on
escalators? There are the little periods of time between doing
other things, the minutes we spend waiting for the unpunctual,
the times of relaxation after meals—and so on. These are
moments in which the mind can recollect the presence of God,
and it may be, offer up a concise prayer. Brother Lawrence
learned to practise the presence of God in this way, when he
was serving as a soldier. "A little lifting up the heart suffices;
a little remembrance of God, one act of inward worship,
though upon a march, and sword in hand, are prayers which,
however short, are nevertheless very acceptable to God." A
person will often excuse his neglect of God by saying, "I have
no time to pray." Are there then no odd moments in the life
of even the most busy person? This is a way of prayer for busy
people; it should not be the only way.

THE REWARDS OF RECOLLECTION

The habit of recollecting the presence of God during the
course of the day has beneficial effects within the Quiet Time,
the special period of prayer. The most common, and to many
the greatest difficulty encountered in prayer is that of wan-

dering thoughts. "I just cannot concentrate. I begin to read the Bible, and my mind goes off at a tangent. I start to pray, and my thoughts wander all over the place." When that happens, there is only one thing we can do *in a* Quiet Time, and that is to keep on recalling the mind without fuss or worry. But there is a good deal to be done about it *outside* the Quiet Time, as Brother Lawrence had discovered. "One way to recollect the mind easily in the time of prayer, and preserve it more in tranquillity, is not to let it wander too far at other times." Can we really expect to concentrate in the quiet room or the church service, if we never bother to think about God throughout the course of the day or the week? Recollection outside the Quiet Time ensures concentration within it. There is, however, a far greater reward, for we "establish ourselves in a sense of God's presence, by continually conversing with Him".[1] Intellectually, we may accept as true the affirmations of the psalmists:

"Nevertheless I am continually with Thee; Thou dost hold my right hand" (Psalm 73: 23).
"Whither shall I go from Thy Spirit?
Or whither shall I flee from Thy presence?
If I ascend to heaven, Thou art there!
If I make my bed in Sheol, Thou art there!" (139: 7, 8).

With our minds we may believe the Divine promises:

"My presence will go with you, and I will give you rest" (Exodus 33: 14).
"Lo, I am with you always, to the close of the age" (Matthew 28: 20).

But it is only by *the practice* of the presence of God, that we *realise* this truth and *appropriate* these promises in experience. Then, substituting his own personal name, a man can write his autobiography in the four words "Enoch walked with God" (Genesis 5: 24).

[1] The non-biblical quotations in this chapter are from *The Practice of the Presence of God*—Brother Lawrence (Bagster's Christian Classics).

SUMMARY

I. Private and public prayer are only a part of devotion, which must include the whole of life.

II. Special prayer-times can enable us to walk with God at all times.

III. Take your prayers out into your life; pray as things happen.

IV. Concise "arrow prayers" help to keep us in touch with God throughout the day.

V. Establish the habit of recollection, of thinking about God during the course of the day.

VI. Set up helpful associations, use practical aids to remind you of God's presence.

VII. Make use of the odd moments for recollection and prayer.

VIII. The habit of recollection helps a person to concentrate during a prayer-time, and to realise in experience the truth of God's perpetual presence.

CHAPTER FIFTEEN

PRAYER AND WORK

THE ACTIVE AND THE CONTEMPLATIVE LIFE

ON one occasion the Lord Jesus Christ was entertained in the home of Lazarus, and his two sisters Martha and Mary, in the village of Bethany just outside Jerusalem. Martha, busily engaged in the preparation of an elaborate meal, was irritated by the behaviour of her younger sister, who sat at the feet of Jesus and kept listening to His word. She protested, "Lord, do you not care that my sister has left me to serve alone? Tell her then to help me." Jesus replied, "Martha, Martha, you are anxious and troubled about many things; one thing is needful. Mary has chosen the good portion which shall not be taken away from her" (Luke 10: 38 to 42). The Lord commends Mary for listening to the word of God; but we must be careful not to misunderstand His reply to Martha. It is certainly a gentle and ironical rebuke of fussiness, and probably means that a simple meal of one course would suffice. But it is not a disparagement of service—it follows the parable of the Good Samaritan!

Among the disciples of Christ, are to be found marked differences of temperament. The contrast may not be so pronounced as in the case of Martha and Mary, but the differences undoubtedly exist. Some people are naturally quiet and contemplative. They like to sit, read, think, meditate, pray. For such the discipline of prayer is comparatively easy. Others, no less devoted to the Lord, prefer to be up and doing. These are the practical people, expressing devotion in action, loyalty in service. What about yourself? To which group do you belong? Where do your sympathies lie, with Martha or with Mary? Most people in the Western world have a sneaking sympathy for Martha! But the best comment on this story has been made by St. Teresa. "To render our Lord a perfect hospitality, Martha and Mary must combine." They must be combined in each one of us. The life of prayer must find expression in service, contemplation in action, worship in work.

WORSHIP AND SERVICE IN THE BIBLE

Martha and Mary are certainly combined throughout the Holy Scriptures, where no distinction is to be found between the worship and the service of God. Both in the Hebrew of the Old and the Greek of the New Testament, one and the same word is translated into English sometimes as "worship", sometimes as "service". Here are two examples of the way in which the Authorised Version and the Revised Standard Version, variously translate the same original. Describing his vision to the crew and passengers of the storm-tossed ship, Paul says, "for this very night there stood by me an angel of the God to whom I belong, and whom I *worship*" (R.S.V.) . . . "God, whose I am and whom I *serve*" (A.V.). The same apostle writes to the Romans, "present your bodies as a living sacrifice, holy and acceptable to God, which is your spiritual *worship*" (R.S.V.) . . . "which is your reasonable *service*" (A.V.). These are both good translations, and both are needed to do full justice to the original meaning (The Acts 27: 23; Romans 12: 1). To worship God is to serve Him; to serve Him is to worship Him. In the Old Testament, the chief act of worship was the offering of sacrifice. But in the New Testament the metaphor of sacrifice is not confined to what we today call "acts of devotion". Not only is it used of the spiritual sacrifices of praise and prayer (I Peter 2: 5), but also of sharing our resources with the needy (Hebrews 13: 16), of money gifts (Philippians 4: 18), of evangelistic activity (Romans 15: 16), and of the dedication of the whole personality to God's service (Romans 12: 1). No distinction is drawn between acts of devotion expressed in praise and prayer, and acts of devotion expressed in service and work. Martha and Mary are combined. The worshipper is the servant of the Lord.

FROM THE MOUNTAIN-TOP TO THE VALLEY

If then, the prayer life is to be fruitful, we must make this combination, or rather exhibit this unity of prayer and service, worship and work, which is found in the Bible. Something is radically wrong, if a healthy person spends a lot of time in prayer, and yet never seeks to express that devotion in the practical service of God and man. It is not according to the example of Christ. He went up the mountain to pray. The enraptured Peter, desiring to prolong the communion with God, wanted to make three dwellings, so that Jesus, Moses and Elijah might *stay* there. The offer was not accepted. A distracted father and his epileptic son were waiting at the foot of the mountain, and Christ went down from intimate prayer to effective service. But while there are some who pray without serving, there are many more nowadays who serve without praying. The modern world is full of folk who are "distracted with much serving, anxious and troubled about many things". Never was there so much ineffective service. Much of it is well-intentioned; yet it is futile, because impotent to deal with the evil in man. The nine apostles who did not pray on the mountain-top, were unable to cast the demon out of the epileptic boy. They had to be told, "this kind cannot be driven out by anything but prayer" (Mark 9: 29). Prayer is the secret of *effective* service. This unity, then, must be maintained both ways. Prayer must issue in service, and service find its inspiration in prayer. True worship must bear fruit in good work, and work itself be transformed into worship.

RIGHT INTENTION

How, in practice, can we maintain and express this unity of prayer and service, of worship and work? Is there not some way, in addition to the practice of the presence of God, by which it is possible to extend the devotional life beyond the Quiet Time, so that it flows into our work, transforms it, and makes it a part of devotion? There is such a way. There exists what George Hebert called "the famous stone, that turneth all to gold". In his book "A Serious Call", William Law institutes "an inquiry into the reason why the generality of Christians fall so far short of the holiness and devotion of Christianity". He comes to the conclusion that "it is because men have not so much as *the intention to please God in all their actions*". In these words we have the open secret of holy living. It is right intention that transforms the common task into Divine service, "that turneth all to gold". Jeremy Taylor in his book *Holy Living*, stresses this same truth. Right intention means "that we should intend and design God's glory in every action we do, whether it be natural or chosen". He adds, "this grace is so excellent, that it sanctifies the most common action of our life, and yet so necessary, that without it the very best actions of our devotion are imperfect and vicious". Not just His prayers, but the whole life of Christ was devotion, because He did *all* things to please God. This should be the single, steady, aim of the Christian. "So, whether you eat or drink, or whatever you do, do all to the glory of God" (I Corinthians 10: 31).

SERVING THE LORD

In many churches, it is customary for the minister to preface the sermon with the words, "in the name of the Father and of the Son and of the Holy Spirit"; it is by His authority and for His glory that I now do this. But ought not a Christian to be able to say that before beginning any job of work? "Whatever your task, work heartily, *as serving the Lord* and not men" (Colossians 3: 23). Not only preaching a sermon, but address-ing a political meeting; not only breaking bread at the Eucharist, but breaking stones to make a road; not only kneeling to pray, but kneeling to scrub the kitchen floor, can be done to the glory of God. The charwoman had grasped this truth when she said, "I put the Lord Jesus Christ into the shine on the door-knobs." Beware of the widespread assumption that some activities are by nature "religious" and "spiritual", while others are ordinary and common. A religious activity may be secular, as when a man preaches a sermon to enhance his own reputation. A common activity may be spiritual, as when Christ washed the feet of His apostles, the menial task of a domestic slave. Brother Lawrence taught us "that our sanctification did not depend upon *changing* our works, but in doing that for God's sake, which we commonly do for our own". And so, whether you are trimming the privet hedge, or writing a letter, cleaning the shoes, or working in a factory, decarbonising your car, or saying your prayers—do all as well as you can, with the intention of pleasing God.

WORSHIP AND WORK

Right intention, doing everything as unto the Lord, breaks down the barrier between work and worship; they become like the two sides of a penny, two aspects of one whole. This is what we find in the Bible.

In the very first recorded act of worship, Cain and Abel offered up to the Lord, the first-fruits of the field and the flock (Genesis 4: 3–5). At the temple a pastoral and agricultural community offered to God the products of work—bread, wine, oil, corn, fruit, sheep, oxen. Worship was offering, and the offering was the fruit of labour. This relationship was preserved in the primitive Eucharist, at which all the people made gifts of bread and wine. Not only in the sanctuary, but in field and factory, in shop and office, in classroom and council chamber, our work is to be offered to God. The offering in church *re-presents* the dedication of all work and service to God. Divine service does not conclude with the Benediction!

"LABORARE EST ORARE"

The ancient Jewish writer Ben-Sira was concerned with the question of how the ordinary working man could live a life of devotion to God. Unlike the scribe who had "opportunity of leisure", the farmer and the artificer, the smith and the potter, together with all those who "maintain the fabric of the world", were busy men, too preoccupied for long periods of prayer and meditation. Yet they also can be devoted to God, for "in the handywork of their craft is their prayer" (Ecclesiasticus 38: 24–34). *Laborare est orare*—to work is to pray. This does *not* mean that bustling activity and hard work are an acceptable substitute for meditation and prayer. After all, Martha was rebuked by Christ for that very mistake. Not all work is prayer, and work may never be a substitute for prayer. But all work done with the intention to please God, is prayer, and is *one* important way in which a busy person can worship. For it is possible to worship with the hand and the brain, as well as with the lips. In the play *The Zeal of Thy House*, Raphael defends Master William the architect of the cathedral, who loves his work and is doing an excellent job, by saying:

"Behold, he prayeth; not with the lips alone,
But with the hand and with the cunning brain
Men worship the Eternal Architect.
So, when the mouth is dumb, the work shall speak
And save the workman. True as mason's rule
And line can make them, the shafted columns rise
Singing like music; and by day and night
The unsleeping arches with perpetual voice
Proclaim in heaven, to labour is to pray."[1]

HOW TO TURN WORK INTO WORSHIP

How can we turn service into prayer, work into worship? This is what is involved.

I. Do all your work with *the right intention*. It was said of Brother Lawrence "that the most excellent method he had found of going to God, was that of doing our common business without any view of pleasing men, and (as far as we are capable) purely for the love of God". Unless this intention is present in our work, our prayers will be lacking in vitality and reality. A man cannot work for himself all week, and then switch over to the worship of God on Sunday. "No one can serve two masters . . . you cannot serve God and mammon" (Matthew 6: 24). This is one of the main reasons why people give up prayer and worship. In the end, you have to serve God everywhere—or nowhere.

II. Do all your work *as well as possible*. Obviously you cannot please God in your work by doing it badly. In the law of Moses there were strict regulations to ensure that the offerings of the people were without blemish. Of course our work cannot be perfect; but it is acceptable when we do our best. No man can do more than his best; no man should do less. It is not possible to work badly and pray well. Shoddy work spoils the devotional life; good work quickens it. Set out then to do everything as well as you possibly can.

"If Jesus built a ship, she would travel trim.
If Jesus roofed a barn, no leaks would be left by Him.
If Jesus made a garden, it would look like Paradise.
If Jesus did my day's work, it would delight His Father's eyes."[2]

[1] *The Zeal of Thy House*—Dorothy L. Sayers (Gollantz).
[2] Source unknown.

III. Practice the presence of God in your work, and *do it in fellowship with Him*. You cannot always be thinking of God when you are working, but you can do so sometimes. When Jesus was criticised for working on the sabbath He said, "My Father is working still, and I am working" (John 5: 17). Remember that God is working all the time, and part of His work is being done in and through you. You can enjoy God's fellowship when working, just as much as in church. Indeed, it was said of Brother Lawrence "that he was *more* united to God in his outward employments, than when he left them for devotion in retirement". Enjoy your work if possible, talk to God occasionally while you are doing it, and remember that you are a fellow-worker with Him.

IV. *Offer your work to God*. Remember that worship is offering and what you offer is your work. You can pray with Wesley:

"Son of the Carpenter receive, this humble work of mine."

Such a prayer may be uttered before starting on a job, or while it is in progress, or when it is completed. Daily work may also be consecrated to God during the Quiet Time, with a prayer for wisdom, strength and skill to do it well. When the offering is dedicated in public worship, offer yourself and the work of the coming week to God.

In all these ways the Martha and the Mary in us can combine, to offer the Lord a perfect hospitality.

> "Work shall be prayer, if all be wrought
> As Thou wouldst have it done;
> And prayer, by Thee inspired and taught
> Itself with work be one."

SUMMARY

I. Prayer and service must be combined in our devotion to the Lord.

II. No distinction is made in the Bible between the worship and the service of God.

III. Prayer without service and service without prayer are alike contrary to the example of Christ.

IV. Work becomes part of the devotional life when it is done with the intention to please God.

   V. We should serve the Lord in all that we do.

  VI. Worship is work offered up to God.

 VII. The layman can concentrate on the worship of God by doing his work for God.

VIII. Work becomes worship when it is done—with the right intention; as well as possible; in fellowship with God; as an offering to God.

CHAPTER SIXTEEN

PRAYER AND LIFE

THE HOLY IS THE COMMON

"THE greatest contribution of the Hebrew to religion is that he did away with it."[1] For the ancient pagan, the sacred was a small area of life, carefully fenced off from the common and the ordinary. The god dwelt in the temple which was holy, and a man went there to worship him, or to consult him through his appointed representative. The temple and its enclosure was sacred; outside all was common. But the living God of the Bible is the Creator of the universe and the Lord of history. As the Creator and Lord of all life, He cannot be fenced off, or confined within the bounds of a special area called "the religious". He is concerned with wages as well as with prayers, with justice as well as with worship, with nations as well as with churches. It follows that devotion to Him must find expression not only in prayers, private or public, but in every part of life. "Prayers, therefore, are so far from being a sufficient devotion, that they are the smallest parts of it. We are to praise God with words and prayers, because it is a possible way of glorifying God, who has given us such faculties, as may be so used. But then as words are but small things in themselves, as times of prayer are but little, if compared with the rest of our lives; so that devotion which consists in times and forms of prayer is but a very small thing, if compared to that devotion which is to appear in every other part and circumstance of our lives."[2]

BALANCED DEVOTION

What does it mean to express devotion in every part of our lives? The Carthusians endeavoured to express a balanced and complete devotion in the three-fold activity or worship,

[1] *Only One Way Left*—George F. Macleod (Iona Community).
[2] *A Serious Call*—William Law.

study and manual work. "This resolving of life into three main divisions—affection, thought, and action, is practically satisfactory. In each of these realms to have some strong central interest will secure the desired equilibrium of the soul. If religion be the central preoccupation of the heart, it will gain in strength, health, and endurance, if it be balanced by some keen discipline of the mind not directly connected with religion; and both will benefit by some outward work of art, skill, or ministration, which calls mainly upon the bodily powers and the practical intelligence, and not directly upon the intellect or the spirit."[1] This maintenance of spiritual balance or equilibrium is of vital importance. One of the outstanding characteristics of the Lord Jesus was the wide range of His interests. He was not a person with a one-track mind, with one absorbing interest called "religion". He was not pietistic or churchy. As is evident from His parables, He was keenly interested in every aspect of life. We can avoid the danger of pietism (not piety, which is a gift of the Spirit), of being self-consciously good, of being too religious in the bad sense, by the deliberate cultivation of non-religious interests. "I want you, just because you long for religion, to continue to cultivate, to cultivate more carefully and lovingly, also the interests, the activities, that are not directly religious. And this, not simply because 'why, of course, we must eat our dinner; of course, we must have our little relaxations'; but, much more, because, without these not directly religious interests and activities, you—however slowly and unperceivedly—lose the material for Grace to work in and on."[2]

HOME, WORK, SOCIETY

Worship, study and work, may be the ideal for a monastic community. But we are in "the race, where the immortal garland is to be run for, not without dust and heat". How can we offer a balanced and complete devotion to the Lord? We must do it within and through the three orders of creation—the family, daily work, and our common life in society. Life begins and is nurtured within the family. Devotion which

[1] *Oil and Wine*—George Tyrrell.

[2] *Letters From Baron Friedrich von Hügel To A Niece*—Edited by Gwendolen Greene (J. M. Dent & Sons, Ltd.).

makes no difference to the way a person lives at home is obviously bogus. Relationship with the Lord should transform the relationships of the family, of husband and wife, parent and child, brother and sister. Prayer should enable a man to take his full share in the joys and the responsibilities of the home. At a certain age, school is left behind, and a man enters the community of labour, the economic order. He takes some part in the processes of production, distribution and consumption, and helps to "maintain the fabric of the world". He earns his living and supports a family, by giving some service to the community. As was indicated in the previous chapter, devotion should be expressed in work well done, to the glory of God. The worker is also a member of society. He must live as a responsible citizen of this world, rendering to Caesar the things that are Caesar's. He should be interested in his locality, in social and civic affairs, in politics and national life. Communion with God should result in "holy worldliness"—responsible participation in the life of society. For withdrawal should be balanced by participation. The worship of God should result in the transformation of the three orders of creation—home, work and society. When this takes place, devotion is both balanced and wholehearted, sane and complete.

WORSHIP AND CONDUCT

Prayer, then, should influence the whole of life, and for the ordinary man today, that means life at home, at work and in society. This is, however, only a way of saying that true prayer bears fruit in *good conduct*. Prayer and righteousness, devotion and lovingkindness, belong together. It was the assumption that they did not belong together, or could be divorced, that roused the indignation of the great Hebrew prophets. Many of their contemporaries imagined that what God required was simply a large number of "acts of devotion". If a sufficient number of sacrifices were offered, according to the prescribed ritual, all would be well, God would be satisfied. These devotional acts, though costly, had no influence upon the conduct of the worshippers. They had become substitutes for right personal relationships, whether domestic, economic or social. But God is not pleased with acts of devotion severed from holy living. He *hates* them. "Your new moons and your appointed feasts my soul hates; they have become a burden to me, I am weary of bearing them . . . cease to do evil, learn to do good; seek justice, correct oppression; defend the fatherless, plead for the widow" (Isaiah 1: 14, 16, 17). Not all prayer is acceptable to God, just because it is prayer. Devotional acts are hateful to God, if they do not bear fruit in justice and lovingkindness. The teaching of the prophets is summed up in the great utterance "behold to obey is better than sacrifice, and to hearken than the fat of rams" (I Samuel 15: 22). This does *not* mean that kindness and social righteousness are an acceptable substitute for worship—the heresy of the modern man. What God requires is obedience, of which worship and service, prayer and kindness, are alike necessary expressions. We must take note, not only of the first and the second, but also of the third part of Micah's justly renowned utterance. "He has showed you, O man, what is good; and what does the Lord require of you but to do justice, and to love kindness, and to walk humbly with your God" (Micah 6: 8).

EXPRESSING DEVOTION IN CONDUCT

We are to express our devotion to the Lord, not only in our prayers, but in our conduct—by the way we carry on at home, at work and in the world. That is right and fitting, and in the case of a true devotion, inevitable. The devotion of a husband to his wife, will find expression in words. They may be words of love or gratitude, of apology or request, corresponding to adoration, thanksgiving, confession and petition in prayer. But a wife would, quite rightly, be doubtful of the genuineness of a love which was confined to verbal expression. The devoted husband also expresses his love in doing. He embodies it in acts of courtesy and kindness, in deeds of helpfulness and service. Words may not be substituted for actions, nor actions for words. Both words and actions are necessary for the full expression of devotion. So it is with loving the Lord—in prayer we speak, in conduct we act out our devotion. Helping with the chores at home, patiently teaching an apprentice his job, designing a house, making a pie for the family of a neighbour who is ill, serving on the local council, can all be acts of devotion to the Lord. And love grows by means of the acts which express it. Doing our love, helps us in speaking our love—just as conversely, prayer is the inspiration for action.

PRAYING AND LOVING

Because God is holy, those who live in communion with Him must walk in newness of life. "You shall be holy, for I am holy" (I Peter I : 15). But there is another reason why our love for Him must be expressed, not only in our prayers, but also in our personal relationships. We have to deal with God Himself in all our dealings with other people. My relationship with God is not just vertical, it is also horizontal. I may ascend to Him up the Jacob's ladder of prayer. He is also present in my neighbour, and I may meet Him there. *I have to deal with Him there.* In the parable of the Last Judgement, the righteous express surprise when they are accepted and commended for having fed and clothed, entertained and visited Christ. Unwilling to enter the eternal kingdom under false pretences, they ask "Lord, when did we see thee?" The King replies, "As you did it to one of the least of these my brethren, you did it to me" (Matthew 25 : 31–46). They had been dealing with Christ Himself, in dealing with their needy brethren. Is this not the most direct way in which we can love the Lord? "No man has ever seen God; if we love one another, God abides in us and His love is perfected in us" (I John 4 : 12). These words were written to those who "believe in the name of His Son Jesus Christ", not to those who deliberately substitute good works for faith. To those who believe and therefore pray, fellowship with God is perfected in love of the brethren. How difficult it is to pray, when our relationships are wrong! Try for example, to pray after a quarrel, or when you have been spiteful in conversation! On the other hand, when we encourage and give, help and serve, how easy it is to pray. Loving helps praying, just as praying helps loving. "He prayeth best who loveth best."

THE THINGS THAT STIR US TO LOVE

By right conduct and by love (they are the same thing) we may express our devotion to God in the world. This love is primarily love for people—primarily, but not only. In all the things which stir and quicken us to love, we may know in experience the presence of God, and express our devotion to Him. We were thinking in Chapter XIV of "the practice of the presence of God". But there are times, many times, when God takes the initiative, and without any effort on our part, discloses Himself to us. All that is required of us, is recognition and love. As George Macdonald says, "whatever wakes my heart and mind, thy presence is, my Lord". The mind may be quickened by some aspect of nature, of art, or of the common life. Edward Wilson of the Antarctic said, "love comes to me by one channel only—the recognition of some beauty, whether mental, moral, or physical; colour or sound or form". A sunset or a symphony, a poem or a song, a deed of heroism or a discovery of science, may quicken the mind to an awareness of God. Listening to an address, reading a book, the devotion of a dog, an unexpected gift, a letter from a friend, any experience, fact or event, may be used by God, may be a stairway down which He comes to us. "He (Christ) knew the error of those philosophers who see nothing between their own lonely selves and God in an infinite distance; for Him man was not a lonely spirit on the earth, lonely in his private search for a far-distant God. God is to be found and seen, not through an illimitable vacancy between Himself and the spirit of man, but in and through all things that stir men to love. He is to be seen in the light of a cottage window as well as in the sun or the stars."[1]

THE CONSECRATION OF THE COMMONPLACE

The true end of the devotional life is the devoted life. Prayers, whether private or public, should transform the life of the home and daily work, the common life of the world, so that all may at last be holy to the Lord. The Jewish people were accustomed to regarding certain places and times, certain objects and persons as especially holy. But the prophet Zechariah looked forward to the time when *everything* in the community would be sacred; when "religion" as a separate sphere, a department of life, would be abolished. "And on that day there shall be inscribed on the bells of the horses, 'holy to the Lord'." Not only the mitre of the high-priest

[1] *Studies in Christianity*—Arthur Clutton (Brock).

upon which these words were inscribed but the common horses in the street—the cars, bicycles and buses of the ancient world—would be sacred to God. Not only the vessels of the altar "but every pot in Judah and Jerusalem shall be sacred to the Lord of hosts". The whole of life, personal, domestic, economic, social, would belong to God, be devoted to His worship and service (Zechariah 14: 20, 21). This should be the aim of the devotional life. We must have our special times and places, our private prayers and church services; but the purpose of these is the consecration of the commonplace. When John of Patmos looked through an open door into heaven, he saw no temple in the new Jerusalem. The entire city was holy of holies. The presence of God had consecrated the whole. The aim of the devotional life has been realised when we can really sing with the seraphim:

Holy, holy, holy, Lord God of hosts,
Heaven and earth are full of thy glory.
Glory be to thee O Lord most high. Amen.

SUMMARY

I. Not a part, but the whole of life must be devoted to the Lord.

II. A true Christian is not just interested in religion, but in the whole of life.

III. We should express our devotion to the Lord in the home, in our daily work, and in the common life of society.

IV. The Holy God requires of His worshippers holiness of life.

V. Devotion must be done as well as said; be expressed moral conduct as well as in prayers.

VI. We can love the Lord by loving our fellow-men.

VII. We can worship God through all the things that stir us to love.

VIII. The purpose of devotion is the consecration of life.

PART TWO

MORNING AND EVENING PRAYERS
FOR ONE MONTH

PREFACE TO THE PRAYERS

THIS diary of personal prayer is designed to help the reader put into practice some of the principles, suggestions, and methods set forth in this book. Praises and Prayers are provided for the mornings and evenings of the thirty-one days of a calendar month. They can be used in sequence, equally well, either with or without reference to the days of the month. The theme of each order is indicated in the title, and the subjects chosen follow the basic pattern of the Christian faith and way of life. Each order provides for the receptive or listening aspect of communion with God, for Scripture Reading and Meditation, as described in Chapter IV. No prepared order can ever exactly fit our circumstances, or give full expression to present desires, aspirations, and needs. That is why a place has been suggested in each order for Extempore Prayer. The written praises and prayers, many of which are from the Scriptures and from various liturgies, can widen the scope of devotion and help us to pray with the Bible and with the Church. The use of both "I" and "we" is deliberate, since Christian prayer is both personal and corporate; in secret, with and for others. Each order is brief, having in mind the limited time available on the average busy day.

ACKNOWLEDGMENTS

THE Scripture quotations (except the Magnificat) are from the *Revised Standard Version* of the Bible, copyrighted 1946 and 1952 by the Division of Christian Education, National Council of Churches, and used by permission.

The text of the *Book Of Common Prayer* is Crown copyright, and the extracts from it are reproduced by permission.

The extracts from the *Prayer Book As Proposed In 1928* have been printed with the permission of the holders of the copyright.

Thanks are also due to the following authors and publishers for permission to include copyright material:

The Committee on Public Worship and Aids to Devotion, the Church of Scotland, for eighteen prayers from the *Book Of Common Order*. (First Day, Morning: Almighty God, whom by searching; Second Day, Evening: Eternal God, in whose perfect kingdom; Fourth Day, Evening: Be present, O merciful God; Fifth Day, Evening: O God, who hast drawn; Sixth Day, Evening: O Lord, I acknowledge; Eighth Day, Evening: Almighty God, who broughtest again; Into Thy hands, O Lord; Tenth Day, Morning: Almighty God, in whom are hid; Tenth Day, Evening: Abide with me; Eleventh Day, Morning: God of all peace; Eleventh Day, Evening: Heavenly Father, who slumberest not; Fourteenth Day, Morning: O God, Lord of all power; Fifteenth Day, Evening: Almighty and most merciful God; Seventeenth Day, Evening: O Lord God almighty; Twentieth Day, Evening: O Thou only wise God; Twenty-second Day, Evening: O God, with whom; Twenty-fifth Day, Evening: O God of hope, fill; Twenty-seventh Day, Evening: O God, who art light.)

The Committee on Public Worship and Aids to Devotion, the Church of Scotland, for four prayers from *Prayers for the Christian Year*. (First Day, Morning: Glory, thanks and praise; Third Day, Evening: O God, who by the cross; Fifth Day, Morning: Most merciful God; Twenty-fifth Day, Evening: Almighty God, we beseech Thee.)

The Oxford University Press, for one prayer from *Daily Prayer*, edited by E. Milner-White and G. W. Briggs. (Fourth Day, Evening: O God, who gavest Thy beloved Son.)

128

The Rev. James Todd and the Independent Press, for one prayer from *Prayers and Services for Christian Festivals*. (Ninth Day, Morning: O God, who hast given.)

The Bishop of Sheffield for one prayer. (Twentieth Day, Morning: Heavenly Father, from whom all fatherhood.)

The Student Christian Movement, for one prayer from *A Book of Prayer for Students*. (Third Day, Evening: O Father of our Lord Jesus Christ.)

The Independent Press for one prayer from *A Book of Services and Prayers*. (Sixth Day, Evening: We pray, O Father.)

Mrs. Harold Anson for one prayer. (Twentieth Day, Morning: O Lord my heavenly Father, be with me.)

I have not been able to trace the source of some of the prayers included. If there has been any infringement of copyright, it has been unintentional, and will, I trust, be pardoned.

OUTLINE OF THE PRAYERS

I. THE ETERNAL FATHER
The Holy Trinity—God the Creator—God the Father—God the King—God the Shepherd—God the Redeemer—God the Judge.

II. THE LORD JESUS CHRIST
The Character of Christ—The Incarnation—The Ministry of Christ—Christ the Teacher—Christ the Healer—Christ the Friend—Christ the Saviour—The Death of Christ—The Resurrection of Christ—The Ascension of Christ—The Priesthood of Christ—Christ the King—The Second Advent of Christ.

III. THE HOLY SPIRIT
The Lord and Giver of Life—The Light of the Holy Spirit—The Fellowship of the Holy Spirit—The Guidance of the Spirit—The Paraclete—The Fruit of the Spirit—The Gifts of the Spirit.

IV. THE HOLY CHURCH
The Church Militant—Worship—The Word of God—Baptism—Holy Communion—Service and Witness—The World Mission of the Church—The Saints—The Church Triumphant.

V. OUR LIFE IN SOCIETY
The Earth—The Sea and the Air—Home and Family—Education—Work—Recreation—Science and Art—The Ministry of Healing—Civic and Social Life—Our Country—The Nations.

VI. CHRISTIAN CHARACTER
Christian Character—Faith—Hope—Love—Joy—Peace—Patience—Kindness—Goodness—Faithfulness—Gentleness—Self Control—Reverence—Gratitude—Self-Examination.

FIRST DAY, MORNING   *THE HOLY TRINITY*

GLORY, thanks, and praise be to the Father, holy and eternal, the Father of our Lord Jesus Christ.

Glory, thanks, and praise be to the holy and eternal Son, the Saviour and Redeemer of the world.

Glory, thanks, and praise be to the holy and eternal Spirit, the Renewer, Sanctifier, and Comforter of our souls.

Glory, thanks, and praise be to the blessed and undivided Trinity, one God for evermore. Amen.

SCRIPTURE READING AND MEDITATION

ALMIGHTY GOD, whom by searching we cannot find out unto perfection, but who in Jesus Christ hast revealed Thyself as Father, and who by Thy Holy Spirit hast borne witness that we are joint-heirs with Christ; help us to confess our faith in Thee our Father by living as Thy children, our faith in Thy Son by following in His steps, and our faith in Thy Holy Spirit by our obedience to His light within our souls; through Jesus Christ our Lord. Amen.

O HEAVENLY FATHER, we pray Thee to bless and protect Thy servants who have gone forth to preach the gospel in distant lands, especially. . . . Give them success in their labours, that Thy way may be known upon earth, Thy saving health among all nations; through Jesus Christ our Lord. Amen.

EXTEMPORE PRAYER

O GOD, bless and help others today, through the prayers I offer, the words I speak, the work I do, the service I give, and the life I live; through Jesus Christ my Lord. Amen.

THE GRACE of the Lord Jesus Christ and the love of God and the fellowship of the Holy Spirit be with us all. Amen.

FIRST DAY, EVENING   *GOD THE CREATOR*

O MOST high, almighty, good Lord God, to Thee belong praise, glory, honour, and all blessing!

Praised be my Lord God with all His creatures, and especially our brother the sun, who brings us the day and who brings us the light; fair is he and shines with a very great splendour; O Lord, he signifies to us Thee.

Praised be my Lord for our sister the moon, and for the stars, the which He hath set clear and lovely in heaven.

Praised be my Lord for our brother the wind, and for air and cloud, calms and all weather, by the which Thou upholdest life in all creatures.

Praised be my Lord for our sister water, who is very serviceable unto us and humble and precious and clean.

Praised be my Lord for our brother fire, through whom Thou givest us light in darkness; and he is bright and pleasant and very mighty and strong.

Praised be my Lord for our mother the earth, the which doth sustain us and keep us, and bringeth forth divers fruits, and flowers of many colours, and grass.

Praised be my Lord for all who pardon one another for His love's sake, and who endure weakness and tribulation.

Praise ye and bless ye the Lord, and give thanks unto Him, and serve Him with great humility. Amen.

SCRIPTURE READING AND MEDITATION

EXTEMPORE PRAYER

I BELIEVE in one God the Father Almighty, Maker of heaven and earth, and of all things visible and invisible.

O GOD, who hast made the earth so fair, and written Thy glory in the heavens, help us inwardly to respond to all that is outwardly true and beautiful, so that, as we pass through things temporal, we may have vision of things eternal; through Jesus Christ our Lord. Amen.

WORTHY art Thou, our Lord and our God, to receive the glory and the honour and the power; for Thou didst create all things, and because of Thy will they were, and were created. Amen.

SECOND DAY, MORNING   *GOD THE FATHER*

IT IS very meet, right, and our bounden duty, that we should at all times, and in all places, give thanks unto Thee, O Lord, holy

Father, almighty, everlasting God. Therefore with angels and archangels, and with all the company of heaven, we laud and magnify Thy glorious name, evermore praising Thee and saying: holy, holy, holy, Lord God of hosts, heaven and earth are full of Thy glory; glory be to Thee, O Lord most high. Amen.

SCRIPTURE READING AND MEDITATION

O GOD, I beseech Thee to send the Spirit of Thy Son Jesus Christ into my heart, that I may cry with faith, love and joy, "Abba, Father". Amen.

O GOD our Father, in whom we live and move and have our being, open our eyes that we may ever behold Thy fatherly presence about us. Draw our hearts to Thee with the power of Thy love. Teach us to be anxious for nothing and, when we have done what Thou has given us to do, help us to leave the issue to Thy wisdom. Take from us doubt and mistrust. Lift our thoughts up to Thee in heaven, and make us to know that all things are possible to us through Thy Son, our Saviour Jesus Christ. Amen.

ALMIGHTY GOD, from whom all fatherhood in heaven and earth is named, grant that the Spirit of wisdom, power, and love may rest upon all Christian parents, that by prayer, precept, and example they may bring up their children in the discipline and instruction of Thy Son, Jesus Christ our Lord. Amen.

EXTEMPORE PRAYER AND THE LORD'S PRAYER

SECOND DAY, EVENING   *GOD THE KING*

BLESSED art Thou, O Lord, the God of Israel our Father, for ever and ever. Thine, O Lord, is the greatness, and the power, and the glory, and the victory, and the majesty; for all that is in the heavens and in the earth is Thine; Thine is the kingdom, O Lord, and Thou art exalted as head above all. Both riches and honour come from Thee, and Thou rulest over all. In Thy hand are power and might; and in Thy hand it is to make great and to give strength to all. And now we thank Thee, our God, and praise Thy glorious name.

I CONFESS to Thee, O God, that in the thoughts of my mind, the desires of my heart, the words of my lips, and the works of my hands, I have sinned against Thee. Have mercy upon me, cleanse me from my sins, and strengthen me in all goodness; through Jesus Christ my Lord. Amen.

SCRIPTURE READING AND MEDITATION

EXTEMPORE PRAYER

O LORD, who has set before us a great hope that Thy kingdom shall come on earth, and hast taught us to pray for its coming: make us ever ready to thank Thee for the signs of its dawning, and to pray and work for the perfect day when Thy will shall be done, on earth as it is in heaven. Amen.

ETERNAL GOD, in whose perfect kingdom no sword is drawn but the sword of righteousness, and no strength known but the strength of love; so guide and inspire, we pray Thee, the work of all who seek Thy kingdom at home and abroad, that all peoples may seek and find their security, not in force of arms, but in the perfect love that casteth out fear, and in the fellowship revealed to us by Thy Son, Jesus Christ our Lord. Amen.

O GOD, I ask Thee to take my hands and work through them, take my lips and speak through them, take my mind and think through it, take my will and make it Thine, take my heart and set it on fire with Thy love; for Jesus Christ's sake. Amen.

THIRD DAY, MORNING   GOD THE SHEPHERD

THE LORD is my shepherd, I shall not want; He makes me lie down in green pastures.

He leads me beside still waters; He restores my soul.

He leads me in paths of righteousness for His name's sake.

Even though I walk through the valley of the shadow of death, I fear no evil; for Thou art with me; Thy rod and Thy staff, they comfort me.

Thou preparest a table before me in the presence of my enemies; Thou anointest my head with oil, my cup overflows.

Surely goodness and mercy shall follow me all the days of my life; and I shall dwell in the house of the Lord for ever.

O LORD our God, open my eyes, that I may behold wondrous things out of Thy law: and let the words of my mouth and the meditation of my heart, be acceptable in Thy sight, O Lord, our Rock and our Redeemer. Amen.

SCRIPTURE READING AND MEDITATION

EXTEMPORE PRAYER

O SHEPHERD of Israel, Thou who leadest Thy people like a flock, I pray for all parents and pastors, teachers and welfare workers. Endue them with wisdom, power, and love, that they may nourish, guide, and protect those committed to their charge. Bless all who go forth to preach, teach, and speak in Thy name, that the other sheep also may hear Thy voice and be brought home to Thy fold, so that there may be one flock, one Shepherd; this I ask through Jesus Christ my Lord. Amen.

O GOD, whose never-failing providence ordereth all things both in heaven and earth: we humbly beseech Thee to put away from us all hurtful things, and to give us those things which be profitable for us; through Jesus Christ our Lord. Amen.

THIRD DAY, EVENING   GOD THE REDEEMER

OUT of the depths I cry to Thee, O Lord! Lord, hear my voice! Let Thy ears be attentive to the voice of my supplications! If Thou, O Lord, shouldst mark iniquities, Lord, who could stand? But there is forgiveness with Thee, that Thou mayest be feared. I wait for the Lord, my soul waits, and in His word I hope; my soul waits for the Lord more than watchmen for the morning. O Israel, hope in the Lord! For with the Lord there is steadfast love, and with Him is plenteous redemption. And He will redeem Israel from all his iniquities.

SCRIPTURE READING AND MEDITATION

O FATHER of our Lord Jesus Christ, who didst graciously send Thy Son to suffer and die for us men and for our salvation: make me truly thankful for this and all Thy benefits:

For Thy long-suffering with the sins and sorrows of men from the beginning even until now:

For the sufferings of Christ in the flesh, and His intercession for mankind in glory:

For the redemption of the world through the pain of the passion and the shame of the cross:

For all who have filled up the sufferings of Christ in their own lives for love of Him and of their fellow-men:

I thank Thee, O God. Amen.

EXTEMPORE PRAYER

O GOD, who by the cross and passion of Thy Son Jesus Christ didst save and deliver mankind; grant that by steadfast faith in the merits of that holy sacrifice we may find help and salvation, and may triumph in the power of His victory; through the same Jesus Christ our Lord. Amen.

BLESSING and honour, and glory, and power, be unto Him that sitteth upon the throne, and unto the Lamb, for ever and ever. Amen.

FOURTH DAY, MORNING   GOD THE JUDGE

BEFORE the glorious throne of Thy majesty, O Lord, and the awful judgement seat of Thy burning love, we Thy people do kneel with cherubim and seraphim and archangels, worshipping, confessing, and praising Thee, Lord of all, Father, Son, and Holy Spirit for ever. Amen.

SEARCH me, O God, and know my heart! Try me and know my thoughts! And see if there be any wicked way in me, and lead me in the way everlasting!

EXTEMPORE PRAYER OF CONFESSION

ALMIGHTY GOD, my heavenly Father, who of Thy great mercy hast promised forgiveness of sins to all who forgive their brethren and with hearty repentance and true faith turn unto Thee; have mercy upon me; pardon and deliver me from all my sins, confirm and strengthen me in all goodness, and bring me to eternal life; through Jesus Christ my Lord. Amen.

SCRIPTURE READING AND MEDITATION

EXTEMPORE PRAYER

O GOD, the Judge of all the earth, let Thy Holy Spirit lead me
through this present world, in holiness and righteousness all
the days of my life. Enable me so to use the time, talents and
possessions entrusted to me, in the service of others and to
Thy glory, that I may at last receive the blessing 'Well done,
good and faithful servant, enter thou into the joy of Thy Lord';
grant this, O merciful Father, through Jesus Christ my Saviour.
Amen.

O GOD our Father, I pray for my family, friends, and fellow-
workers. Help them amid the chequered experiences of this
life always to serve Thee faithfully and with a cheerful courage,
and so bring them to the end of their days with a quiet mind;
through Jesus Christ our Lord. Amen.

THE LORD'S PRAYER

FOURTH DAY, EVENING   THE CHARACTER OF CHRIST

SCRIPTURE READING AND MEDITATION

THANKS be to Thee, O God, for Thine unspeakable gift, Jesus
Christ our Lord. For His holy incarnation and lowly birth,
for His growth in stature, wisdom, and grace, for His home
and work at Nazareth:
   I thank Thee, O God.
For His perfect life and example, for the words He spoke for
my instruction and guidance, for His deeds of power and love,
and for His character full of grace and truth:
   I thank Thee, O God.
For His agony in the Garden of Gethsemane, for His patience
and meekness in the Judgement Hall, for His precious sufferings
and death upon the cross, for the perfect and sufficient sacrifice
He offered there for the sins of the world:
   I thank Thee, O God.
For His glorious resurrection and ascension, for His continual

intercession and rule at Thy right hand, for His gift of the Holy Spirit and for the blessed hope of His advent in glory:
I thank Thee, O God. Amen.

EXTEMPORE PRAYER OF INTERCESSION

O GOD, who gavest Thy beloved Son, the holy One and just, the meek and lowly in heart, to be the pattern of our living: help us, who must be measured by His measure and compared with His beauty, both to long and to strive after His likeness, that all men may know that we have been with Jesus; to the glory of Thy name. Amen.

BE PRESENT, O merciful God, and protect us through the silent hours of this night, so that we who are wearied by the changes and chances of this fleeting world may repose upon Thy eternal changelessness; through Jesus Christ our Lord. Amen.

FIFTH DAY, MORNING   *THE INCARNATION*

MY SOUL doth magnify the Lord, and my spirit hath rejoiced in God my Saviour. For He hath regarded the lowliness of His handmaiden. For, behold, from henceforth all generations shall call me blessed. For He that is mighty hath magnified me, and holy is His name. And His mercy is on them that fear Him throughout all generations. He hath showed strength with His arm; He hath scattered the proud in the imagination of their hearts. He hath put down the mighty from their seat; and hath exalted the humble and meek. He hath filled the hungry with good things, and the rich He hath sent empty away. He remembering His mercy hath holpen His servant Israel, as He promised to our forefathers, Abraham and his seed for ever.

SCRIPTURE READING AND MEDITATION

EXTEMPORE PRAYER

FOR the Word who was with Thee in the beginning, through whom all things were made, who was made flesh and dwelt among us, full of grace and truth: I thank Thee, O God. Amen.

Most merciful God, for whose chosen handmaid and her holy Babe there was no room in the inn at Bethlehem; help us all by Thy Spirit to make more room for the Christ in our common days, that His peace and joy may fill our hearts, and His love flow through our lives to the blessing of others, for His name's sake. Amen.

I BELIEVE in one Lord Jesus Christ, the only-begotten Son of God, begotten of His Father before all worlds, God of God, Light of Light, Very God of Very God, begotten, not made, being of one substance with the Father, by whom all things were made; who for us men, and for our salvation, came down from heaven, and was incarnate by the Holy Spirit of the Virgin Mary, and was made man.

LORD GOD, keep me steadfast in this faith, today and always; through the same Thy Son Jesus Christ. Amen.

FIFTH DAY, EVENING   THE MINISTRY OF CHRIST

PRAISE be to Thee, O God, who through Thy Son Jesus Christ hast revealed Thyself to the world.
Praise be to Thee, O God, that the light of the gospel of the glory of Christ, who is the image of God, has shined upon them that believe.
Blessed be the Lord God of Israel, for He hath visited and redeemed His people: to give light to them that sit in darkness, and in the shadow of death, and to guide our feet into the way of peace. Amen.

O GOD, who didst command the light to shine out of darkness, shine into my heart, to give the light of the knowledge of Thy glory in the face of Jesus Christ. Amen.

SCRIPTURE READING AND MEDITATION

EXTEMPORE PRAYER

O GOD, who didst anoint Thy Son Jesus Christ with the Holy Spirit and with power, who went about doing good and healing all that were oppressed by the devil; enable me by the same

Spirit to follow in His steps and to do those good works which Thou hast prepared beforehand, that I should walk in them; grant this through Jesus Christ my Lord. Amen.

O BLESSED SAVIOUR, who wast pleased Thyself to be reckoned amongst the craftsmen, bless all who labour with their hands, especially . . . . that their work may be done for Thy honour, and rewarded with Thy approval. Amen.

O GOD, who hast drawn over weary day the restful veil of night, enfold us in Thy heavenly peace. Lift from our hands our tasks, and bear in Thy bosom the weight of our burdens and sorrows; that in untroubled slumber we may press our weariness close to Thy strength, and win from Thee new power for the morrow's labours, through Jesus Christ our Lord. Amen.

SIXTH DAY, MORNING   *CHRIST THE TEACHER*

I AM the Bread of Life: if anyone eats of this bread he will live forever.

    Glory be to Thee, O Christ.

I am the Light of the World: he who follows Me will not walk in darkness, but will have the light of life.

    Glory be to Thee, O Christ.

I am the Door of the Sheep: if anyone enters by Me, he will be saved.

    Glory be to Thee, O Christ.

I am the Good Shepherd: the Good Shepherd lays down His life for the sheep.

    Glory be to Thee, O Christ.

I am the Resurrection and the Life: he who believes in Me, though he die, yet shall he live, and whoever lives and believes in Me shall never die.

    Glory be to Thee, O Christ.

I am the True Vine: you are the branches. Abide in Me and I in you.

    Glory be to Thee, O Christ.

I am the Way, and the Truth, and the Life: no one comes to the Father but by Me.

    Glory be to Thee, O Christ. Amen.

LORD JESUS, grant me grace both to hear and to do these words of Thine, that I may be like the wise man who built his house upon the rock; for Thy name's same. Amen.

O LORD, our heavenly Father, almighty and everlasting God, who hast safely brought us to the beginning of this day; defend us in the same with Thy mighty power; and grant that this day we fall into no sin, neither run into any kind of danger; but that all our doings may be ordered by Thy governance, to do always that is righteous in Thy sight; through Jesus Christ our Lord. Amen.

SCRIPTURE READING AND MEDITATION

EXTEMPORE PRAYER, AND THE LORD'S PRAYER

SIXTH DAY, EVENING   *CHRIST THE HEALER*

SCRIPTURE READING AND MEDITATION

O LORD, I acknowledge my shortcomings and failures, and humbly confess my errors and sins, especially . . . But forasmuch as Thou delightest to show mercy, I beseech Thee to pardon and absolve me, to deliver me from the burden of my transgression, and to release me from the power of sin; through Jesus Christ my Saviour. Amen.

EXTEMPORE PRAYER OF THANKSGIVING

GRANT to me, O God, I beseech Thee, health of body and soundness of mind; that I may work efficiently, serve faithfully, and live joyfully, to the glory of Thy holy name. Amen.

ALMIGHTY GOD, whose blessed Son Jesus Christ went about doing good, and healing all manner of disease among the people: continue, we beseech Thee, this His gracious work among us, especially in the hospitals and infirmaries of our land. Cheer, heal, and sanctify the sick, especially . . . Grant to all physicians, surgeons, and nurses, both wisdom and skill, sympathy and patience; and send Thy blessing on all who labour to prevent suffering and to forward Thy purposes of love; through Jesus Christ our Lord. Amen.

WE PRAY, O Father, for all who have gone to other lands to heal and to save; for those who have taken to the mission fields and places of need the knowledge and skill Thou hast granted to them. Grant that, bearing the Saviour's presence with them, they may heal the sick, cleanse the lepers, and restore sight to the blind; through Jesus Christ our Lord. Amen.

LIGHTEN our darkness, we beseech Thee, O Lord; and by Thy great mercy defend us from all perils and dangers of this night; for the love of Thy only Son, our Saviour, Jesus Christ. Amen.

SEVENTH DAY, MORNING   CHRIST THE FRIEND

SCRIPTURE READING AND MEDITATION

O LORD, open Thou my lips, and my mouth shall shew forth Thy praise.

FOR my parents, family, and relatives, for all that they mean to me and have done for me:
    I thank Thee, O God.
For all those who have helped me by word, deed, and example:
    I thank Thee, O God.
For all my friends, both old and new, and for all the joy of loving and being loved:
    I thank Thee, O God.
For the visible fellowship of Thy Church, and the invisible communion of saints:
    I thank Thee, O God.
For the friendship of the Lord Jesus Christ, who laid down His life for us, and who lives to be with us for ever:
    I thank Thee, O God. Amen.

O LORD JESUS CHRIST our Saviour, who hast called us to be Thy friends: help me by Thy Spirit so to trust and obey Thee, that I may grow daily in the knowledge and love of Thee; for Thy name's same. Amen.

O LORD GOD, whose will and joy it is that Thy children love one another: bless my friendships, that they may be made happy and kept pure by Thine unseen presence, now and at all times; through Jesus Christ my Lord. Amen.

EXTEMPORE PRAYER

HELP me, O God, to express my love for people today, whether by prayers or gifts, by words or deeds; and through my love make manifest and real to them Thy great love in Jesus Christ my Lord. Amen.

MAY THY grace and peace, O God, be with me this day. Amen.

SEVENTH DAY, EVENING   CHRIST THE SAVIOUR

SCRIPTURE READING AND MEDITATION

O SAVIOUR of the world, the Son, Lord Jesus, stir up Thy strength and help us, we humbly beseech Thee.
By Thy cross and precious blood Thou hast redeemed us; save us and help us, we humbly beseech Thee.
Thou didst save Thy disciples when ready to perish; hear us and save us, we humbly beseech Thee.
Let the pitifulness of Thy great mercy loose us from our sins, we humbly beseech Thee.
Make it appear that Thou art our Saviour and mighty Deliverer; O Save us that we may praise Thee, we humbly beseech Thee.
Draw near according to Thy promise, from the throne of Thy glory; look down and hear our crying, we humbly beseech Thee.
Come again and dwell with us, O Lord Christ Jesus; abide with us for ever, we humbly beseech Thee.
And when Thou shalt appear with power and great glory, may we be made like unto Thee in Thy glorious kingdom.
        Thanks be to Thee, O Lord; Alleluia.

EXTEMPORE PRAYER

ALMIGHTY and everlasting God, who, of Thy tender love towards mankind, hast sent Thy Son, our Saviour Jesus Christ, to take upon Him our flesh and to suffer death upon the cross, that all mankind should follow the example of His great humility; mercifully grant that we may both follow the example of His patience, and also be made partakers of His resurrection; through the same Jesus Christ our Lord. Amen.

O Lord, who neither slumberest nor sleepest, be pleased in Thy mercy to watch over us this night. Guard us while waking and defend us while sleeping, that when we wake we may watch with Christ, and when we sleep we may rest in peace. Grant this, for His sake, our only Saviour and Redeemer. Amen.

EIGHTH DAY, MORNING   THE DEATH OF CHRIST

O Saviour of the world, who by Thy cross and precious blood hast redeemed us:
Save us and help us, we humbly beseech Thee, O Lord.
All we like sheep have gone astray, we have turned every one to his own way:
Have mercy upon us.
We have crucified Thee, the Lord of glory, afresh, and put Thee to an open shame:
Have mercy upon us.
Lamb of God, that takest away the sins of the world:
Have mercy upon us.
Lamb of God, that takest away the sins of the world:
Grant us Thy peace. Amen.

For Jesus Christ our Saviour; for His celebration of the Last Supper in the Upper Room; for His agony in the Garden of Gethsemane; for His patience and meekness in the Judgement Hall; for His stripes by which we are healed:
I thank Thee, O God.
For His precious sufferings and death upon the cross, on which He gave Himself for us, a fragrant offering and perfect sacrifice unto Thee:
I thank Thee, O God.

Worthy is the Lamb who was slain, to receive power and wealth and wisdom and might and honour and glory and blessing. Amen.

Almighty God, who hast given Thine only Son to be unto us both a sacrifice for sin, and also an example of godly life: give us grace that we may always most thankfully receive that His inestimable benefit, and also daily endeavour ourselves to follow the blessed steps of His most holy life; through the same Jesus Christ our Lord. Amen.

SCRIPTURE READING AND MEDITATION

EXTEMPORE PRAYER, AND THE LORD'S PRAYER

EIGHTH DAY, EVENING   THE RESURRECTION OF CHRIST

SCRIPTURE READING AND MEDITATION

PRAISE be to Thee, O Father almighty, who didst raise up Thy Son from the dead and give Him glory, that our faith and hope might be in Thee.

Praise be to Thee, O Lord Jesus Christ, the resurrection and the life, who by Thy glorious resurrection didst bring life and immortality to light.

Praise be to Thee, O Holy Spirit, who dost shed abroad the love of Christ in our hearts, and makest us to rejoice in the hope of glory. Amen.

ALMIGHTY GOD, who broughtest again from the dead our Lord Jesus, the glorious Prince of Salvation, with everlasting victory over sin and the grave; grant us power, we beseech Thee, to rise with Him to newness of life, that we may overcome the world with the victory of faith, and have part at last in the resurrection of the just; through the merits of the same risen Saviour, who liveth and reigneth with Thee and the Holy Spirit, ever one God, world without end. Amen.

O FATHER of mercies and God of all comfort, I pray for all who have been bereaved, especially . . . Manifest to them Thy presence, uphold them by Thy power and comfort them by Thy Spirit. Grant them steadfast faith and sure hope in Him who is the resurrection and the life; even Jesus Christ our Lord. Amen.

EXTEMPORE PRAYER

INTO Thy hands, O Lord, I commend myself and all whom I love, beseeching Thee to keep us under the shadow of Thy wings. Drive far from us every evil thing; give Thine angels charge over us; guard us ever, in life and in death, that whether we wake or sleep we may live together with Thee; through Jesus Christ our Lord. Amen.

NINTH DAY, MORNING   THE ASCENSION OF CHRIST

THOU art the King of Glory, O Christ; Thou art the everlasting Son of the Father.

When Thou tookest upon Thee to deliver man, Thou didst not abhor the Virgin's womb.

When Thou hadst overcome the sharpness of death, Thou didst open the Kingdom of Heaven to all believers.

Thou sittest at the right hand of God in the glory of the Father.

We believe that Thou shalt come to be our Judge: we therefore pray Thee help Thy servants, whom Thou hast redeemed with Thy precious blood.

Make them to be numbered with Thy saints in glory everlasting.

SCRIPTURE READING AND MEDITATION

EXTEMPORE PRAYER

O GOD, who hast given Thy Son to be Head over all things to the Church: we pray Thee to strengthen its faith, to enrich its life, and to confirm its witness through all the world. Unite Thy people in the bond of Thy love, as they acknowledge one Lord, one faith, and one baptism; and so endue them with power from on high that with all boldness they may proclaim Thy word. Grant that Thy Church may hear and obey the command to preach the gospel to every creature; and hasten the day when all men shall confess Him to be the Saviour, to whom Thou hast given all power in heaven and on earth— even Jesus Christ our Lord. Amen.

O GOD, whose most dearly beloved Son was, by Thy mighty power, exalted into the heavens, that He might prepare a place in Thy kingdom of glory for them that truly love Thee, so lead and uphold me, O merciful Lord, that I may both follow the most holy steps of His life on earth and may enter with Him hereafter into Thy everlasting rest; that where He is, I may be also; through the merits of the same Jesus Christ my Lord. Amen.

NINTH DAY, EVENING   THE PRIESTHOOD OF CHRIST

SCRIPTURE READING AND MEDITATION

O ETERNAL GOD, who hast called Thy Church to be a holy priesthood, to offer spiritual sacrifices: grant to us all the aid of Thy Holy Spirit, that our praises and prayers, our offerings and the oblation of our lives, may be acceptable unto Thee; through Jesus Christ our Lord. Amen.

O LORD JESUS CHRIST, the one Mediator between God and man, who livest for ever to make intercession for us; grant that by Thy all-powerful prayers I may be delivered from evil, strengthened in goodness, conformed to Thy likeness, and equipped for Thy service; for Thy name's sake. Amen.

O LORD JESUS CHRIST, I join my prayers to Thine, on behalf of my family . . . my friends . . . my fellow-workers . . . the members of my local Church . . . beseeching Thee to fulfil in them all the purpose of Thy redeeming love. Amen.

EXTEMPORE PRAYER

FOR the intercession of our Lord Jesus Christ in glory:
    I thank Thee, O God.
For the Holy Spirit who helps us in our infirmity and teaches us how to pray:
    I thank Thee, O God.
For the prayers of the saints; for all who have prayed for me in the past; for all who are praying for me now:
    I thank Thee, O God.
For the privilege of direct access into Thy presence through Christ in the Spirit; and for all the answers I have received to my prayers:
    I thank Thee, O God, through Jesus Christ my Lord. Amen.

GRANT, we beseech Thee, almighty God, unto us who know that we are weak, and who trust in Thee because we know that Thou art strong, the gladsome help of Thy lovingkindness, both here in time and hereafter in eternity. Amen.

TENTH DAY, MORNING   CHRIST THE KING

THANKS be to Thee, O God our Father, who hast set Thy Son Jesus Christ upon the throne of Thy kingdom, and hast crowned Him with glory and honour.

Thanks be to Thee, O Christ our Saviour, who hast borne our manhood into heaven itself, and livest for ever to make intercession for us.

Thanks be to Thee, O Holy Spirit our Helper, the giver of life and light, through whom alone we confess that Jesus Christ is Lord, to the glory of God the Father. Amen.

ALMIGHTY GOD, in whom are hid all the treasures of wisdom and knowledge; open my eyes that I may behold wondrous things out of Thy law; and give me grace that I may clearly understand and heartily choose the way of Thy commandments; through Jesus Christ my Lord. Amen.

SCRIPTURE READING AND MEDITATION

EXTEMPORE PRAYER

ETERNAL FATHER, who didst give Thine only Son the name most dear to Thee and needful for mankind, betokening not His majesty, but our salvation: we pray Thee to set the name of Jesus high above every name, and to plant in every heart the love of the only Saviour; who liveth and reigneth with Thee and the Holy Spirit, one God, world without end. Amen.

ALMIGHTY GOD, from whom all thoughts of truth and peace do proceed; kindle, we pray Thee, in the hearts of all men the true love of peace, and guide with Thy pure and peaceable wisdom those who take counsel for the nations of the earth; that in tranquillity Thy kingdom may advance and go forward, till the earth be filled with the knowledge of Thy love; through Jesus Christ our Lord.

LORD JESUS, my King, rule my life today, and grant that in all my thoughts and desires, my words and deeds, I may worship and serve Thee; for Thy dear sake. Amen.

TENTH DAY, EVENING   THE SECOND ADVENT OF CHRIST

SCRIPTURE READING AND MEDITATION

I BELIEVE . . . He shall come again with glory to judge both the living and the dead; whose kingdom shall have no end.

JESUS, remember me when you come in your kingly power. Amen.

ALMIGHTY GOD, give us grace that we may cast away the works of darkness, and put upon us the armour of light, now in the time of this mortal life, in which Thy Son Jesus Christ came to visit us in great humility; that in the last day, when He shall come again in His glorious majesty to judge both the living and the dead, we may rise to the life immortal, through Him who liveth and reigneth with Thee and the Holy Spirit, now and ever. Amen.

O GOD, I praise Thee for the gift of Jesus Christ. For His lowly birth; for His hidden years; for His wise words and mighty deeds; for His character full of grace and truth; for His sacrifice on the cross; for His glorious resurrection and ascension; for the hope of His advent in glory; and for His kingdom which has no end: I thank Thee, O God. Amen.

EXTEMPORE PRAYER

ABIDE with me, O Lord, for it is toward evening, and the day is far spent. Teach me to number my days, that I may apply my heart unto wisdom; and because I know neither the day nor the hour of Thy coming, give me grace to live in such a state that I shall not fear to die therein; so that when Thou comest, whether at even, or at midnight, or in the morning, Thou mayest find me ready; who livest and reignest with the Father and the Holy Spirit, world without end. Amen.

ELEVENTH DAY, MORNING   *THE LORD AND*
                                 GIVER OF LIFE

Come, Holy Ghost, our souls inspire,
And lighten with celestial fire.
Thou the anointing Spirit art,
Who dost Thy seven-fold gifts impart.

They blessed unction from above,
Is comfort, life, and fire of love.
Enable with perpetual light
The dulness of our blinded sight.

Anoint and cheer our soiled face
With the abundance of Thy grace.
Keep far our foes, give peace at home:
Where thou art guide, no ill can come.

Teach us to know the Father, Son,
And Thee, of both, to be but one.
That, through the ages all along,
This may be our endless song;
Praise to Thy eternal merit,
Father, Son, and Holy Spirit

SCRIPTURE READING AND MEDITATION

GOD of all peace and encouragement, who didst gloriously fulfil the great promise of the Gospel by sending down the Holy Spirit on the day of Pentecost, to establish the Church as the house of His continual presence and power among men; mercifully grant unto us, we beseech Thee, this same gift of the Spirit, to renew, illuminate, refresh, and sanctify our souls; to be over us and around us like the light and dew of heaven, and to be in us evermore as a well of water springing up unto everlasting life; through Jesus Christ our Lord. Amen.

O HOLY Spirit, Lord and Giver of life, I pray for those known to me who do not believe, especially . . . Grant that by Thy unseen operation in their hearts they may be made alive to God through Jesus Christ my Lord. Amen.

EXTEMPORE PRAYER AND THE LORD'S PRAYER

ELEVENTH DAY, EVENING   *THE LIGHT OF THE*
HOLY SPIRIT

O GOD, who according to the promise of Jesus Christ Thy Son, didst send the Spirit of truth unto Thy people; grant that He may teach us all things, guide us into all truth, open to us the Scriptures, and take the things of Christ and show them unto us; for Thy name's sake. Amen.

SCRIPTURE READING AND MEDITATION

GOD, who didst teach the hearts of Thy faithful people, by the sending to them the light of Thy Holy Spirit; grant us by the same Spirit to have a right judgement in all things, and evermore to rejoice in His holy comfort; through the merits of Christ Jesus our Saviour, who liveth and reigneth with Thee, in the unity of the same Spirit, one God, world without end. Amen.

O GOD, who by Thy Spirit in our hearts dost lead men to desire Thy perfection, to seek for truth, and to rejoice in beauty; illumine, we pray Thee, and inspire all thinkers, writers, artists, and craftsmen; that in whatsoever is true and pure and lovely, Thy name may be hallowed and Thy kingdom come on earth; through Jesus Christ our Lord. Amen.

EXTEMPORE PRAYER

HEAVENLY FATHER, who slumberest not nor sleepest; I commend to Thy gracious care and keeping myself and all who belong to me. I thank Thee for the light of this day, and now for the restful night. Lift from my mind the burdens of waking hours; visit my body with refreshing sleep; through the darkness keep me safe and undefiled. And wake me to meet tomorrow's duties in strength of body and vigour of mind, with peace in my soul and courage in my heart; through Jesus Christ my Lord. Amen.

TWELFTH DAY, MORNING   *THE FELLOWSHIP*
OF THE HOLY SPIRIT

WE PRAISE Thee, O God; we acknowledge Thee to be the Lord. All the earth doth worship Thee; the Father everlasting.

To Thee all angels cry aloud; the heavens, and all the powers
therein.
To Thee cherubim, and seraphim, continually do cry,
Holy, holy, holy; Lord God of Sabaoth;
Heaven and earth are full of the majesty of Thy glory.
The glorious company of the apostles praise Thee;
The goodly fellowship of the prophets praise Thee;
The noble army of martyrs praise Thee.
The holy Church throughout all the world doth acknowledge
Thee;
The Father of an infinite majesty;
Thine honourable, true, and only Son;
Also the Holy Ghost the Comforter.

SCRIPTURE READING AND MEDITATION

O GOD, who hast called me into the fellowship of Thy Son:
grant me grace, I beseech Thee, to continue steadfastly in the
apostles' teaching and fellowship, in the breaking of bread
and the prayers; through the same Jesus Christ my Lord.
Amen.

O LORD JESUS CHRIST, who didst pray for Thy disciples that they
might be one, even as Thou art one with the Father: draw us
to Thyself, that in common love and obedience to Thee we
may be united to one another in the fellowship of the one
Spirit, and the world may believe that Thou art Lord, to the
glory of God the Father. Amen.

EXTEMPORE PRAYER

THE GRACE of the Lord Jesus Christ and the love of God and
the fellowship of the Holy Spirit be with us all. Amen.

TWELFTH DAY, EVENING   *THE GUIDANCE OF*
THE SPIRIT

LEAD me Lord, lead me in Thy righteousness, make Thy way
plain before my face. For it is Thou, Lord, Thou Lord only
that makest me dwell in safety. Amen.

I Confess my iniquity, I am sorry for my sin. Do not forsake me, O Lord! O my God, be not far from me! Make haste to help me, O Lord, my salvation!

SCRIPTURE READING AND MEDITATION

For today, for health and food, for strength and guidance, for home and work, for love and fellowship: I thank Thee, O God. Amen.

O God, by whom the meek are guided in judgement, and light riseth up in darkness for the godly; grant us in our doubts and uncertainties, the grace to ask what Thou wouldest have us to do; that the Spirit of wisdom may save us from all false choices, and that in Thy light we may see light, and in Thy straight path may not stumble; through Jesus Christ our Lord. Amen.

O God, I beseech Thee, grant to all Ministers of State and Members of Parliament the wisdom and guidance of Thy Holy Spirit; that all their decisions may promote the well-being of this nation, to the glory of Thy holy name. Amen.

EXTEMPORE PRAYER

O Lord, support us all the day long of this troublous life, until the shadows lengthen and the evening comes, and the busy world is hushed, the fever of life is over, and our work done; then, O Lord, in Thy mercy, grant us safe lodging, a holy rest, and peace at the last; through Jesus Christ our Lord. Amen.

THIRTEENTH DAY, MORNING   THE PARACLETE

For the gift of the Holy Spirit, who at creation moved upon the face of the deep, spoke of old to our fathers by the prophets, and at Pentecost descended as in tongues of living fire upon the Church:
   I thank Thee, O God.
For the presence and work of Thy Holy Spirit in the Church, inspiring worship, creating fellowship and spreading the gospel throughout the world:
   I thank Thee, O God.

For the Holy Spirit who dwells in me, quickening me, rebuking me for sin, strengthening me in weakness, guiding me in perplexity, comforting me in sorrow, teaching me to pray, revealing to me the things of Christ and changing me into His likeness:

I thank Thee, O God, through Jesus Christ my Lord. Amen.

SCRIPTURE READING AND MEDITATION

O GOD, forasmuch as without Thee we are not able to please Thee: mercifully grant that Thy Holy Spirit may in all things direct and rule our hearts; through Jesus Christ our Lord. Amen.

GRANT Thy blessing, almighty Father, to all my occupations this day, both when I am alone and when I am with others. Give me humble thoughts concerning myself, that I may count it all honour to be permitted to serve Thee. Inspire me with the grace of self-sacrifice and self-forgetfulness, that I may think first of Thee and of my brethren. In all that I do may I look upward for Thy blessing, and remember that it is Thou only, O Lord, who workest in me by the Holy Spirit, both to will and to do; through Jesus Christ my Lord. Amen.

EXTEMPORE PRAYER AND THE LORD'S PRAYER

THIRTEENTH DAY, EVENING   THE FRUIT OF THE SPIRIT

SCRIPTURE READING AND MEDITATION

ALMIGHTY and most merciful God, I acknowledge and confess that I have sinned against Thee in thought, and word, and deed: that I have not loved Thee with all my heart and soul, with all my mind and strength; and that I have not loved my neighbours as myself. I beseech Thee, O God, to be forgiving to what I have been, to help me to amend what I am, and of Thy mercy to direct what I shall be; so that the love of goodness may ever be first in my heart, and I may follow unto my life's end in the steps of Jesus Christ my Lord. Amen.

O GOD our Father, grant that we Thy servants, beholding with unveiled face the glory of our Saviour Jesus Christ, may be changed into His likeness from glory to glory by the Lord the Spirit; by His unseen operation in our hearts may Christ be formed in us, and all the fruit of the Spirit be made manifest in our lives; even love, joy, peace, patience, kindness, goodness, faithfulness, gentleness, self-control. This we ask through the merits and mediation of Thy Son Jesus Christ our Lord. Amen.

O GOD, I pray for all those I have met today, especially for . . . May Thy Holy Spirit help them to know and to do Thy will. Guard them from all evil and danger; incline them to all virtue and goodness. Grant to them quiet and refreshing sleep this night, and the strength, wisdom, and joy of the Spirit all through the coming day; for Jesus Christ's sake. Amen.

EXTEMPORE PRAYER

DEFEND, O Lord, us Thy servants with Thy heavenly grace, that we may continue Thine for ever, and daily increase in Thy Holy Spirit more and more, until we come to Thy everlasting kingdom; through Jesus Christ our Lord. Amen.

FOURTEENTH DAY, MORNING   *THE GIFTS OF THE SPIRIT*

MOST merciful God, shed abroad Thy Holy Spirit upon me: that He may cleanse my heart, enlighten my mind, kindle my affections, and enable me to offer acceptable worship unto Thee; through Jesus Christ my Lord. Amen.

SCRIPTURE READING AND MEDITATION

O ALMIGHTY GOD, by whose breath I have received life, let Thy Holy Spirit rest upon me in His seven-fold energy; the Spirit of wisdom and understanding, the Spirit of counsel and might, the Spirit of knowledge and true godliness, and fill me with the Spirit of holy fear, now and for evermore. Amen.

ETERNAL FATHER, from whom cometh every good and perfect gift, I pray for all who guide and inspire the thoughts of the people; for authors and journalists, for poets, artists, and musicians; and for all who provide instruction and entertainment through radio and television; grant to them all vision and strength, inspiration and skill, that they may deepen our insights, make glad our hearts, and crown our common life with truth and beauty; through Jesus Christ our Lord. Amen.

EXTEMPORE PRAYER

O GOD, Lord of all power and might, preserver of all Thy creatures; keep me this day in health of body and soundness of mind, in purity of heart and cheerfulness of spirit, in contentment with my lot and charity with my neighbour; and further all my lawful undertakings with Thy blessing. In my labours strengthen me: in my pleasures purify me: in my difficulties direct me: in my perils defend me: in my troubles comfort me: and supply all my needs, according to the riches of Thy grace in Christ Jesus my Lord. Amen.

FOURTEENTH DAY, EVENING · THE CHURCH MILITANT

SCRIPTURE READING AND MEDITATION

ALMIGHTY GOD, I lift up my heart in gratitude to Thee for Thy Church, which Thou hast built upon the one sure foundation, Jesus Christ my Lord. I praise Thee for the worship of the sanctuary, for the Holy Scriptures, for the preaching and teaching of the word, for the sacraments of Baptism and the Lord's Supper, and all the means of grace. I thank Thee for the fellowship of Thy people, for the faithful service and witness of dedicated lives, for all the work and influence of Thy Church throughout the world and for our communion with those who have entered into Thy rest. Unto Thee, O God, in the unity of the Holy Spirit, be praise and glory in the Church, throughout all ages, through Jesus Christ our Lord. Amen.

WE COMMEND to Thee, almighty God, the whole Christian Church throughout the world. Bless all in every place who call on the name of our Lord Jesus Christ. May the grace and power of the Holy Spirit fill every member, so that all the company of Thy faithful people may bear witness for Thee on the earth. Look in mercy on the errors and confusions of our time, and draw the hearts of all believers nearer to the Lord Jesus Christ. If it be good in Thy sight, heal the outward divisions of Thy people, disposing the wills of all to a true union of order in the truth, for the work of the one Lord. And above all we pray for the unity of the Spirit, by whom alone we are guided into all truth; through Jesus Christ our Lord. Amen.

EXTEMPORE PRAYER

THE LORD has granted His lovingkindness in the daytime; and for this cause now in the night season do I sing of Him, and make my prayer unto the God of my life. Let my prayer be set forth in Thy sight as incense; and let the lifting up of my hands be an evening sacrifice, now and always. Amen.

FIFTEENTH DAY, MORNING   *WORSHIP*

O come, let us sing to the Lord;
let us make a joyful noise to the rock of our salvation!
Let us come into His presence with thanksgiving;
let us make a joyful noise to Him with songs of praise!
For the Lord is a great God,
And a great King above all gods.
In His hand are the depths of the earth;
the heights of the mountains are His also.
The sea is His, for He made it;
for His hands formed the dry land.
O come, let us worship and bow down,
let us kneel before the Lord, our Maker!
For He is our God,
and we are the people of His pasture,
and the sheep of His hand.

SCRIPTURE READING AND MEDITATION

DELIVER us, O almighty God, when we draw nigh to Thee, from coldness of heart and wanderings of mind: that with steadfast thought and kindled desire we may worship Thee in spirit and in truth; through Jesus Christ our Lord. Amen.

O GOD, help me to worship Thee today, not only with my lips, but with my life; not only in praise and prayer, but in loving-kindness and service. Grant that all my work may be prayer, and all my life be praise, because I do all things unto Thee and for Thy glory. Amen.

EXTEMPORE PRAYER

O THOU, who art the light of the minds that know Thee, the joy of the hearts that love Thee, and the strength of the wills that serve Thee; help us so to know Thee that we may truly love Thee, so to love Thee that we may fully serve Thee, whose service is perfect freedom. Through Jesus Christ our Lord. Amen.

FIFTEENTH DAY, EVENING   THE WORD OF GOD

ALMIGHTY and most merciful God, who hast given the Bible to be the revelation of Thy great love to man, and of Thy power and will to save him; grant that my study of it may not be made in vain by the callousness or carelessness of my heart, but that by it I may be confirmed in penitence, lifted to hope, made strong for service, and above all filled with the true knowledge of Thee and of Thy Son Jesus Christ. Amen.

SCRIPTURE READING AND MEDITATION

EXTEMPORE PRAYER

O LORD GOD ALMIGHTY, who didst endue Thine apostles with singular gifts of the Holy Spirit, so that they proclaimed Thy word with power; grant unto all those who are set to minister and preach in Thy holy name, the same Spirit of wisdom, love and power; that the truth Thou givest them to declare may search the conscience, convince the mind, and win the heart of those who hear it, and the glory of Thy kingdom be advanced; through Jesus Christ our Lord. Amen.

GRANT Thy blessing, O God, to all those who translate, print, and circulate the Holy Scriptures; may Thy Spirit endue them with true knowledge and skill, with patient zeal and love, that

Thy word may speed on and triumph; through Jesus Christ our Lord. Amen.

THY WORD is a lamp to my feet, and a light to my path. Thanks be to Thee, O Lord. Amen.

O LORD, my God, refresh me with quiet sleep, wearied with the day's work; that being assisted with the help my weakness needs, I may be devoted to Thee both in body and mind; through Jesus Christ my Lord. Amen.

SIXTEENTH DAY, MORNING   *BAPTISM*

SCRIPTURE READING AND MEDITATION

FOR THE baptism of our Lord Jesus Christ in the Jordan:
For the command of our Lord Jesus Christ to His apostles:
Go therefore and make disciples of all nations, baptising them in the name of the Father and of the Son and of the Holy Spirit:
For all those who have been baptised in His name, and have kept the faith:
For my own baptism in the name of the Father, the Son, and the Holy Spirit:

> I thank Thee, O God, through Jesus Christ my Lord. Amen.

I BELIEVE in God the Father almighty, Maker of heaven and earth. And in Jesus Christ His only Son our Lord, who was conceived by the Holy Spirit, born of the Virgin Mary, suffered under Pontius Pilate, was crucified, dead, and buried, He descended into Hades, the third day He rose again from the dead, He ascended into heaven, and sitteth on the right hand of God the Father almighty, from whence He shall come to judge the living and the dead. I believe in the Holy Spirit; the holy catholic Church; the communion of saints; the forgiveness of sins; the resurrection of the body, and the life everlasting. Amen.

GRANT, O Lord, that as we are baptised into the death of Thy Son our Saviour Jesus Christ, so by continual mortifying our corrupt affections we may be buried with Him; and that through the grave, and gate of death, we may pass to our joyful resurrection; for His merits, who died, and was buried, and rose again for us, Thy Son Jesus Christ our Lord. Amen.

O GOD of hope, I pray for all converts and beginners in the Christian way, especially . . . Fill them with all joy and peace in believing, so that by the power of the Holy Spirit they may abound in hope: through Jesus Christ our Lord. Amen.

EXTEMPORE PRAYER

SIXTEENTH DAY, EVENING   HOLY COMMUNION

SCRIPTURE READING AND MEDITATION

WHAT shall I render to the Lord for all His bounty to me?
I will lift up the cup of salvation and call on the name of the Lord.
O Lord, I am Thy servant; Thou hast loosed my bonds.
I will offer to Thee the sacrifice of thanksgiving and call on the name of the Lord.
I will pay my vows to the Lord in the presence of all His people.
Praise the Lord!

HOLY FATHER, I give thanks to Thee for the sacrament instituted by our Lord Jesus Christ, that we might show forth His death and rejoice in His resurrection, until He comes in glory. Grant that I may always approach the Lord's Table with sincere purpose, deep penitence, true faith, and kindled devotion. Enable me to join in the sacrifice of praise and thanksgiving with my whole heart, and in union with my Saviour, to offer myself unto Thee. Open my eyes to the vision of Thy love, and grant that feeding on Christ by faith, I may be strengthened with might by the Holy Spirit. I ask this for the sake of Him who loved me and gave Himself for me, even Jesus Christ my Lord and Saviour. Amen.

O GOD, before whose altar there is neither far nor near but one eternal Presence, I commend to Thy gracious keeping all everywhere whom Thou hast united with me in bonds of love and friendship, especially . . . beseeching Thee to hold them with me in Thy holy and blessed fellowship; through Jesus Christ my Lord. Amen.

THE LORD almighty grant us a quiet night and a perfect end. Amen.

Father, into Thy hands I commit my spirit. Amen.

SEVENTEENTH DAY, MORNING   SERVICE AND WITNESS

O GOD our Father, who hast bidden the light to shine out of darkness, and hast again wakened us from sleep to praise Thy goodness and ask for Thy grace. Accept now the sacrifice of our worship and thanksgiving, and grant unto us all such requests as may be wholesome for us. Make us to be children of the light, and of the day, and heirs of Thine everlasting inheritance. Remember, according to the multitude of Thy mercies, Thy whole Church; all who join with us in prayer; all our brethren by land or sea or wheresoever they be throughout Thy vast dominion who stand in need of Thy grace and succour. Pour out upon them the riches of Thy mercy; so that being redeemed in soul and body and steadfast in faith, we may ever praise Thy wonderful and holy name; through Jesus Christ our Lord. Amen.

SCRIPTURE READING AND MEDITATION

EXTEMPORE PRAYER

ALMIGHTY and everlasting God, by whose Spirit the whole body of the Church is governed and sanctified; receive our supplications and prayers, which we offer before Thee for all estates of men in Thy holy Church, that every member of the same, in his vocation and ministry, may truly and godly serve Thee; through our Lord and Saviour Jesus Christ. Amen.

O GOD, bless through me those I shall meet this day. Grant that by my words I may enlighten and encourage, and by my deeds strengthen and serve them. Help me both by lip and by life to bear witness to Thy Son, my Saviour Jesus Christ. Amen.

Now To Him who by the power at work within us is able to do far more abundantly than all that we ask or think, to Him be glory in the Church and in Christ Jesus to all generations, for ever and ever. Amen.

SEVENTEENTH DAY,   *THE WORLD MISSION*
EVENING   *OF THE CHURCH*

SCRIPTURE READING AND MEDITATION

O LORD Jesus Christ, who hast commanded us to make disciples of all nations; may Thy Spirit inspire, strengthen, and direct me, so that by my prayers, my gifts and my labours, I may make Thee known to others, and lead them to trust Thee as Saviour and serve Thee as King in the fellowship of Thy Church; for Thy name's sake. Amen.

O GOD our Saviour, who willest that all men should be saved and come to the knowledge of the truth, prosper we pray Thee, our missionaries who labour in distant lands, especially . . . Protect them in all perils by land, sea, and air, support them in loneliness and in the hour of trial; give them grace to bear faithful witness unto Thee and endue them with burning zeal and love, that they may turn many to righteousness and finally obtain a crown of glory; through Jesus Christ our Lord. Amen.

O GOD, who hast made of one blood all nations of men to dwell on the face of the earth, and didst send Thy Son Jesus Christ to preach peace to them that are afar off, and to them that are nigh: grant that all the peoples of the world may feel after Thee and find Thee; and hasten, O Lord, the fulfilment of Thy promise, to pour out Thy Spirit upon all flesh; through Jesus Christ our Lord. Amen.

EXTEMPORE PRAYER

O LORD GOD ALMIGHTY, who hast lit the day with the sun's light, and brightened the night with shining stars; enlighten our souls for ever with the healing beams of the Sun of Righteousness who is risen upon us; and so preserve us at all times in the doing of Thy will, that at the last we may shine as the stars for ever and ever. Grant this for the honour of Thine only Son, Jesus Christ our Lord. Amen.

EIGHTEENTH DAY, MORNING   *THE SAINTS*

ALMIGHTY GOD, I give Thee hearty thanks for the wonderful grace and virtue declared in all Thy saints, who have been the chosen vessels of Thy grace, and the lights of the world in their several generations.

For the prophets and apostles, the evangelists and martyrs; for their flaming zeal and heroic deeds; for their faith and love; for their loyalty to Christ our Lord in life and death:

I thank Thee, O God.

For those who have enriched the world with truth and beauty; for the wise and good of every land and age, who by teaching and life have given light to their fellow-men:

I thank Thee, O God.

For the saints of our own land who stand before Thee, and for the many lamps their holiness hath lit; for all those who have laboured and made sacrifice for freedom, good government and just laws, for those who won the liberty of faith and worship in which we live:

I thank Thee, O God.

For those I have myself known and honoured, who taught me by word and guided me by example, who loved, shielded, and helped me, especially for. . . .

I thank Thee, O God, through Jesus Christ my Lord. Amen.

O ALMIGHTY GOD, who hast knit together Thine elect in one communion and fellowship, in the mystical body of Thy Son Jesus Christ our Lord; grant us grace so to follow Thy blessed saints in all virtuous and godly living, that we may come to those unspeakable joys, which Thou hast prepared for them that unfeignedly love Thee; through the same Jesus Christ our Lord, who liveth and reigneth with Thee and the Holy Spirit, one God, world without end. Amen.

SCRIPTURE READING AND MEDITATION

EXTEMPORE PRAYER AND THE LORD'S PRAYER

EIGHTEENTH DAY, EVENING   *THE CHURCH*
                                 TRIUMPHANT

SCRIPTURE READING AND MEDITATION

BLESSED be the God and Father of our Lord Jesus Christ!
By His great mercy we have been born anew to a living hope
through the resurrection of Jesus Christ from the dead, and to
an inheritance which is imperishable, undefiled and unfading.
Thanks be to God. Alleluia.

O GOD, who hast prepared for them that love Thee such good
things as pass man's understanding; pour into our hearts such
love toward Thee, that we, loving Thee above all things, may
obtain Thy promises, which exceed all that we can desire;
through Jesus Christ our Lord, to whom with Thee and the
Holy Spirit, be all honour and glory, world without end.
Amen.

O GOD, Giver of life and Conqueror of death, I remember
before Thee with a grateful heart, all those dear to me who have
entered into Thy nearer presence, especially . . . . Grant that
their memory and example may inspire me to a better life.
Keep me in unbroken fellowship with them here, and bring me
hereafter to dwell with them in the blessed home of everlasting
light and love; through Jesus Christ my Lord. Amen.

HAVE mercy, O God, upon all who are passing through the
valley of the shadow of death, that they may know Thy presence
with them and awake to behold Thy face; through Him who
is the resurrection and the life, Jesus Christ our Lord. Amen.

EXTEMPORE PRAYER

Now TO the blessed and only Sovereign, the King of kings and
Lord of lords, who alone has immortality and dwells in unap-
proachable light, whom no man has ever seen or can see—to
Him be honour and eternal dominion. Amen.

NINETEENTH DAY, MORNING   *THE EARTH*

SCRIPTURE READING AND MEDITATION

O GOD, we thank Thee for this universe, our great home; for
its vastness and its riches, and for the manifoldness of the life

which teems upon it and of which we are part. We praise Thee for the arching sky and the blessed winds, for the driving clouds and the constellations on high. We praise Thee for the salt sea and the running water, for the everlasting hills, for the trees, and for the grass under our feet. We thank Thee for our senses by which we can see the splendour of the morning, and hear the jubilant songs of love, and smell the breath of the springtime. Grant us, we pray Thee, a heart wide open to all this joy and beauty, and save our souls from being so steeped in care or so darkened by passion that we pass heedless and unseeing when even the thornbush by the wayside is aflame with the glory of God. Amen.

O GOD, I pray for all those who work on the land, especially. . . . Grant that they may be aware of Thy presence and power in creation, may understand Thy laws, and co-operate with Thy wise ordering of the world. Bless the earth with fertility and so prosper their labours, that the needs of all Thy children may be supplied; for Thy name's sake. Amen.

O GOD, who hast made all things, the flowers and trees and the green grass, the sea, the sky, the stars, the birds, and all living things: and hast made man in Thine own image, that he might know who is the Creator of all these things; open my eyes to see Thee everywhere and glorify Thee in all Thy works; through Jesus Christ my Lord. Amen.

EXTEMPORE PRAYER AND THE LORD'S PRAYER

NINETEENTH DAY, EVENING   THE SEA AND THE AIR

Bless the Lord, O my soul!
O Lord my God, Thou art very great!
Thou art clothed with honour and majesty,
Who coverest Thyself with light as with a garment,
Who hast stretched out the heavens like a tent,
Who makest the clouds Thy chariot,
Who ridest on the wings of the wind,
Who makest the winds Thy messengers,
fire and flame Thy ministers.
O Lord, how manifold are Thy works!

In wisdom hast Thou made them all;
the earth is full of Thy creatures.
Yonder is the sea, great and wide,
which teems with things innumerable,
living things both small and great.
There go the ships,
and Leviathan which Thou didst form to sport in it.
May the glory of the Lord endure for ever,
May the Lord rejoice in His works.

SCRIPTURE READING AND MEDITATION

O ETERNAL LORD GOD, who alone spreadest out the heavens, and rulest the raging of the sea: be pleased to receive into Thy protection all those who go down to the sea in ships and occupy their business in great waters. Preserve them both in body and soul; prosper their labours with good success; in all time of danger be their defence, and bring them to the haven where they would be; through Jesus Christ our Lord. Amen.

ALMIGHTY GOD, who makest the clouds Thy chariot and walkest upon the wings of the wind; I remember before Thee this night all those who travel by air to distant places of the earth. Grant strength and courage, skill and sound judgement to all pilots and air-crews, and overshadow them and all those committed to their charge with Thy loving providence and mighty protection. May the sense of Thy presence and the knowledge of Thy fatherly love be with them amidst the wonders of the sky; I ask this for the sake of Jesus Christ my Lord. Amen.

EXTEMPORE PRAYER AND THE LORD'S PRAYER

TWENTIETH DAY, MORNING   HOME AND FAMILY

O GOD my Father, from whom every family in heaven and on earth is named, accept my hearty thanks for my home and for all the blessings and gifts freely bestowed upon me within it. I praise Thee for life and health, for food and clothing, for duty and leisure. I bless Thee for all the love and affection, the joy and humour, the discipline and responsibility of family life. I thank Thee for our house, for the shelter, amenities and comforts it provides, and for all that is useful and beautiful within it. Accept my gratitude and thanksgiving, through Jesus Christ my Lord. Amen.

SCRIPTURE READING AND MEDITATION

HEAVENLY FATHER, from whom all fatherhood in heaven and earth is named: bless, I beseech Thee, all children, and give to their parents, and to all in whose charge they may be, Thy Spirit of wisdom and love: so that the home in which they grow up may be to them an image of Thy kingdom, and the care of their parents a likeness of Thy love; through Christ my Lord. Amen.

O LORD, my heavenly Father, be with me in my home during the coming day. Make me to be loving and patient in my own family, forgiving others, as I remember how much I myself need to be forgiven. Keep me from all hastiness of temper, and from all want of thoughtfulness for others in little things. Make me more ready to give than to receive; and grant that in our home Thy holy law of love may reign, bringing to us a foretaste of Thy kingdom, where Thy love shall be the joy of Thy people for ever. Amen.

EXTEMPORE PRAYER

O GOD, who knowest us to be set in the midst of so many and great dangers, that by reason of the frailty of our nature we cannot always stand upright; grant to us such strength and protection, as may support us in all dangers, and carry us through all temptations; through Jesus Christ our Lord. Amen.

TWENTIETH DAY, EVENING   EDUCATION

MAY THY Spirit, O God, who proceeds from Thee, illumine my mind, and as Thy Son has promised, lead me into all truth; through my Lord Jesus Christ. Amen.

SCRIPTURE READING AND MEDITATION

EXTEMPORE PRAYER

O MERCIFUL GOD, grant that I may eagerly desire, carefully search out, truthfully acknowledge, and ever perfectly fulfil all things which are pleasing to Thee; to the praise and glory of Thy name. Amen.

FOR THE garnered wisdom of the past; for all recent discoveries and new knowledge:
      I thank Thee, O God.
For all that I am learning through the written word; for the Holy Scriptures; for all good books both old and new; for our public libraries; for all wise and devoted authors and journalists:
      I thank Thee, O God.
For all that I am learning through the spoken word; in Church and class; through radio and television; through personal conversation and fellowship:
      I thank Thee, O God, through Jesus Christ my Lord. Amen.

O THOU only wise God, our Saviour, in whom are hid all the treasures of wisdom and knowledge; we beseech Thee to illuminate all universities, colleges, and schools, with light that cometh from above; that those who teach may be taught of Thee, and those who learn may be led by the Spirit; and grant that by the increase of knowledge Thy truth may be confirmed, and Thy glory manifested; through Jesus Christ our Lord. Amen.

LOOK down, O merciful Father, from Thy heavenly throne, illuminate the darkness of this night with Thy celestial brightness, and from the sons of light banish the deeds of darkness; through Jesus Christ our Lord. Amen.

TWENTY-FIRST DAY, MORNING   *WORK*

> Forth in Thy name, O Lord, I go,
>   My daily labour to pursue,
> Thee, only Thee, resolved to know
>   In all I think, or speak, or do.

The task Thy wisdom has assigned
   Oh, let me cheerfully fulfil;
In all Thy works Thy presence find,
   And prove Thy good and perfect will.
Thee may I set at my right hand,
   Whose eyes my inmost secrets see;
And labour on at Thy command,
   And offer all my works to Thee.
For Thee delightfully employ
   What'er Thy bounteous grace hath given,
And run my even course with joy,
   And closely walk with Thee to heaven.

SCRIPTURE READING AND MEDITATION

SHOW me, O God, the way of patient industry: that, honouring and praising Thee in the work of my hands, and learning the dignity of honest labour, I may be faithful in small and humble tasks, a good comrade to my fellows, and brave to fight against all that may hinder fulness of life; through Jesus Christ my Lord. Amen.

ALMIGHTY FATHER, who by Thy Son Jesus Christ hast sanctified labour to the welfare of mankind: prosper, we pray Thee, the industries of this land, and all who are engaged therein; that, being shielded in their hardships and dangers, and receiving their due reward, they may praise Thee by living according to Thy will; through Jesus Christ our Lord. Amen.

EXTEMPORE PRAYER

GRANT to me, O Lord, an evenness of spirit, that I may not be too much elated by success, nor too much cast down by disappointment, for Christ's sake. Amen.

TWENTY-FIRST DAY, EVENING   *RECREATION*

SCRIPTURE READING AND MEDITATION

O GOD most merciful:
For all the good things of life I have failed to appreciate and enjoy, forgive me;

For all the times I have been glum and despondent, when I should have been cheerful and gay, forgive me;
For all the times I have continued to read, listen to, look at, or share in that which was unwholesome and evil, forgive me;
For all my failures to share in and contribute to the innocent fun and pleasures of others, forgive me;
Through Jesus Christ my Saviour. Amen.

OUR HEAVENLY FATHER, who giveth us richly all things to enjoy, I thank Thee for all that makes life glad and joyful. I praise Thee for the loveliness of earth, sky, and sea, and for all the joys of the open air. I bless Thee for all who provide our recreation through newspapers, magazines, and books, through radio and television, through music and song, through films and plays, through sport and entertainment. I thank Thee for daily leisure, for the weekly day of rest, and for my annual holiday. I praise Thee for my own special interests, hobbies, and recreations, for. . . . To Thee, the Author and Giver of all good things, I lift up my heart in gratitude; through Jesus Christ my Lord. Amen.

O GOD, we pray for all those who provide for our recreation and entertainment. Inspire, illumine, and enable them with the Spirit of truth and goodness, of beauty and gladness, that in all our pleasures we may be refreshed and recreated for Thy worship and service; through Jesus Christ our Lord. Amen.

EXTEMPORE PRAYER AND THE LORD'S PRAYER

TWENTY-SECOND DAY, MORNING   SCIENCE AND ART

O all ye works of the Lord, bless ye the Lord:
O ye angels of the Lord, bless ye the Lord:
    Praise Him, and magnify Him for ever.
O ye sun, moon and stars, bless ye the Lord:
O ye summer and winter, O ye days and nights, bless ye the Lord:
    Praise Him, and magnify Him for ever.
O let the earth bless the Lord:
    Yea, let it praise Him, and magnify Him for ever.

O ye seas and floods, O all ye that move in the waters, bless
ye the Lord:
O ye fowls of the air, O ye beasts and cattle, bless ye the Lord:
Praise Him, and magnify Him for ever.
O ye children of men, O ye servants of the Lord, bless ye
the Lord:
O ye souls of the righteous, O ye holy and humble men of
heart, bless ye the Lord:
Praise Him, and magnify Him for ever. Amen.

SCRIPTURE READING AND MEDITATION

EXTEMPORE PRAYER

O GOD, who since the creation of the world hast clearly revealed Thy eternal power and deity in the things that have been
made; enlighten with Thy Spirit all men of science, that as
they study nature, they may reverence Thee. Grant that the
new knowledge and power which has been entrusted to us
through their labours may be used with responsibility toward
Thee, for the welfare of all mankind; through Jesus Christ our
Lord. Amen.

O ETERNAL GOD, the fount of all truth and beauty, grant inspiration, vision, and skill to all artists, musicians and craftsmen, that with colour, sound, and form they may beautify our
common life and make glad our hearts, through Jesus Christ
our Lord. Amen.

GRANT us, O Lord, to pass this day in gladness and peace,
without stumbling and without stain; that reaching the even-
tide victorious over all temptation, we may praise Thee, the
eternal God, who art blessed, and dost govern all things, world
without end. Amen.

TWENTY-SECOND DAY, EVENING   *THE MINISTRY*
OF HEALING

BLESS the Lord, O my soul; and all that is within me, bless His
holy name!
Bless the Lord, O my soul, and forget not all His benefits,

who forgives all your iniquity, who heals all your diseases, who redeems you life from the Pit, who crowns you with steadfast love and mercy, who satisfies you with good as long as you live, so that your youth is renewed like the eagle's.
Bless the Lord, all His works, in all places of His dominion.
Bless the Lord, O my soul!

SCRIPTURE READING AND MEDITATION

O God, Giver of health and healing, I pray for all those who are sick, whether in body or in mind, especially . . . Grant, if it be Thy will, that by Thy mighty power they may be delivered from sickness and restored to health. Give to them confidence and courage, patience and peace, and sustain and sanctify them by Thy Holy Spirit; through Jesus Christ my Lord. Amen.

O Father of mercies, and God of all comfort, who hast made man's body to be a temple of the Holy Spirit: sanctify, we pray Thee, all those whom Thou hast called to study and practice the art of healing the sick, and the prevention of disease and pain. Strengthen them with Thy life-giving Spirit, that by their sacred ministry the health of Thy people may be established; through Thy Son, Jesus Christ our Lord. Amen.

EXTEMPORE PRAYER

O God, with whom there is no darkness, but the night shineth as the day; keep and defend me and all Thy children, in soul and body, during the coming night. Make us to rest in the peace of a good conscience, in the hope of a better life, in the faith of Thy providence, and in the comfort of Thy love; through Jesus Christ our Lord. Amen.

TWENTY-THIRD DAY, MORNING   CIVIC AND SOCIAL LIFE

It is good to give thanks to the Lord,
   to sing praises to Thy name, O most High;
to declare Thy steadfast love in the morning,
   and Thy faithfulness by night,

to the music of the lute and the harp,
   to the melody of the lyre.
For Thou, O Lord, hast made me glad by Thy work;
   at the works of Thy hands I sing for joy.
How great are Thy works, O Lord!
   Thy thoughts are very deep!

GLORY be to the Father, and to the Son, and to the Holy
Spirit; as it was in the beginning, is now, and ever shall be,
world without end. Amen.

O MERCIFUL FATHER, I confess to Thee my negligence and sin
as a citizen. I have been excessively concerned about my
rights and have often neglected my responsibilities. I have
been over-sensitive about the wrongs which affect me, and
have shown an easy acquiescence in wrongs done to others.
My concern for social righteousness has been feeble and fitful.
I have lacked the courage to oppose that which is evil, and the
zeal to strive for that which is good. My life at home, at work,
and in society, has not always commended the gospel of Christ.
Forgive me, cleanse and deliver me from all evil, and so confirm and strengthen me in all goodness, that I may henceforth
do Thy will; through Jesus Christ my Lord. Amen.

SCRIPTURE READING AND MEDITATION

EXTEMPORE PRAYER

O ETERNAL GOD, our heavenly Father, who hast given us Thy
abiding citizenship in heaven, and, in the days of our pil-
grimage, a citizenship upon earth; give us Thine aid, as we
journey to that heavenly city, so faithfully to perform the
duties which befall us on the way, that at the last we may be
found worthy to enter into Thy rest; through Jesus Christ our
Lord. Amen.

TWENTY-THIRD DAY, EVENING   OUR COUNTRY

SCRIPTURE READING AND MEDITATION

ETERNAL GOD, the Father of all mankind, I give Thee humble
and hearty thanks for the good land Thou hast given to us,
and for all Thy blessings upon us as a nation and people. I

praise Thee for the sea and the fertile earth, for quiet villages and busy towns, for our homes and schools, for our sports and industries. I bless Thee for just laws and good institutions, for our heritage of freedom and culture, for all our national heroes and saints and for the stirring history of our race. Above all, I thank Thee for the Churches of our land, for their worship and fellowship, for their witness and service at home and overseas. For all Thy great goodness to us in the past and at this present time, accept my gratitude and thanksgiving; through Jesus Christ our Lord. Amen.

MAY THY mercy and blessing, O Father of all, rest upon our land and nation: upon all the powers which Thou hast ordained over us; our Queen, and all in authority under her; the Ministers of State, the great councils of the nation, and all judges and magistrates; that we may live a quiet and peaceable life in all godliness and honesty. Rule the hearts of men in all classes of our people, and draw all together in true brotherhood and sympathy; through Jesus Christ our Lord. Amen.

EXTEMPORE PRAYER

TEACH us, good Lord, to serve Thee as Thou deservest; to give and not to count the cost; to fight and not to heed the wounds; to toil and not to seek for rest; to labour and not to ask for any reward, save that of knowing that we do Thy will; through Jesus Christ our Lord. Amen.

I WILL lay me down in peace and take my rest;
For it is Thou only, O Lord, that makest me dwell in safety.
Amen.

TWENTY-FOURTH DAY, MORNING   THE NATIONS

May God be gracious to us and bless us
and make His face to shine upon us,
that Thy way may be known upon earth,
Thy saving power among all nations.
Let the peoples praise Thee, O God;
let all the peoples praise Thee!
Let the nations be glad and sing for joy,

for Thou dost judge the peoples with equity
and guide the nations upon earth.
Let the peoples praise Thee, O God;
let all the peoples praise Thee!
The earth has yielded its increase;
God, our God, has blessed us.
God has blessed us;
let all the ends of the earth fear Him.

SCRIPTURE READING AND MEDITATION

O GOD, in whose kingdom power is always at the service of
love, grant that we, the soldiers of Jesus Christ, may maintain
and show forth in the cause of peace, the military virtues of
courage, endurance, discipline, and obedience, that thy kingdom may advance and triumph; through Jesus Christ our
Lord. Amen.

ALMIGHTY GOD, the Father of all mankind, let Thy blessing
rest upon all the work of the United Nations Organization.
Grant Thy wisdom and guidance to those who confer together
and make decisions. Help them to execute justice, to maintain
peace and order, to remove fear and suspicion, and to give
effective help to those who are in need. Make Thy way known
upon earth, Thy saving power among all nations; through
Jesus Christ our Lord. Amen.

EXTEMPORE PRAYER

ETERNAL GOD, in whose will is our peace, I commend to Thee
the needs of all the world: where there is hatred, give love;
where there is injury, pardon; where there is distrust, faith;
where there is despair, hope; where there is darkness, light;
through Jesus Christ our Lord. Amen.

TWENTY-FOURTH DAY, EVENING   *CHRISTIAN CHARACTER*

SCRIPTURE READING AND MEDITATION

Blessed are the poor in spirit, for theirs is the kingdom of
heaven.
Grant me this grace, I beseech Thee, O Lord.

Blessed are those who mourn, for they shall be comforted.
    Grant me this grace, I beseech Thee, O Lord.
Blessed are the meek, for they shall inherit the earth.
    Grant me this grace, I beseech Thee, O Lord.
Blessed are those who hunger and thirst after righteousness,
for they shall be satisfied.
    Grant me this grace, I beseech Thee, O Lord.
Blessed are the merciful, for they shall obtain mercy.
    Grant me this grace, I beseech Thee, O Lord.
Blessed are the pure in heart, for they shall see God.
    Grant me this grace, I beseech Thee, O Lord.
Blessed are the peacemakers, for they shall be called sons of
God.
    Grant me this grace, I beseech Thee, O Lord.
Blessed are those who are persecuted for righteousness' sake,
for theirs is the kingdom of heaven.
    Write these words in my heart, I beseech Thee, O Lord.

O ALMIGHTY GOD, who alone canst order the unruly wills and
affections of sinful men: grant unto Thy people that they may
love the thing which Thou commandest, and desire that which
Thou dost promise; that so, among the sundry and manifold
changes of the world, our hearts may surely there be fixed,
where true joys are to be found; through Jesus Christ our
Lord. Amen.

EXTEMPORE PRAYER

Our help is in the name of the Lord:
Who made heaven and earth.
The Lord almighty grant us a quiet night:
and a perfect end.
Save us, O Lord, waking, guard us sleeping:
that awake we may watch with Christ,
and asleep we may rest in peace.
Thanks be to God. Amen.

TWENTY-FIFTH DAY, MORNING   *FAITH*

I bind unto myself today, the strong name of the Trinity,
By invocation of the same, the Three in One, and One in
  Three.
I bind this day to me for ever, by power of faith, Christ's
  Incarnation;
His baptism in the Jordan river; His death on Cross for my
  salvation;
His bursting from the spiced tomb; His riding up the
  heavenly way;
His coming at the day of doom; I bind unto myself today.
I bind unto myself today, the power of God to hold and lead,
His eye to watch, His might to stay, His ear to hearken to
  my need.
The wisdom of my God to teach, His hand to guide, His
  shield to ward,
The Word of God to give me speech, His heavenly host to
  be my guard.
I bind unto myself the name, the strong name of the Trinity,
By invocation of the same, the Three in One and One in
  Three,
Of whom all nature hath creation, Eternal Father, Spirit,
  Word.
Praise to the Lord of my salvation: salvation is of Christ the
  Lord.

SCRIPTURE READING AND MEDITATION

O LORD Jesus Christ, our only Saviour, help me to trust in
Thee with all my heart, for pardon and strength, for wisdom
and righteousness, for salvation and eternal life, this day and
always. Amen.

O MERCIFUL GOD, who hast made all men, and hatest nothing
that thou hast made, nor would'st the death of a sinner, but
rather that he should be converted and live; have mercy upon
Thine ancient people the Jews, and upon all who have not
known Thee, or who deny the faith of Christ crucified; take
from them all ignorance, hardness of heart, and contempt of
Thy word; and so fetch them home, blessed Lord, to Thy fold,
that they may be made one flock under one Shepherd, Jesus
Christ our Lord. Amen.

EXTEMPORE PRAYER

ALMIGHTY and everlasting God, give unto us the increase of faith, hope, and love; and, that we may obtain that which Thou dost promise, make us to love that which Thou dost command; through Jesus Christ our Lord. Amen.

TWENTY-FIFTH DAY, EVENING   HOPE

SCRIPTURE READING AND MEDITATION

O let my mouth be filled with Thy praise;
That I may sing of Thy glory and honour all day long.
Turn Thy face from my sins, O Lord;
and put out all my misdeeds.
Make me a clean heart, O God;
and renew a right spirit within me.
Cast me not away from Thy presence;
and take not Thy Holy Spirit from me.
O give me the comfort of Thy help again;
and stablish me with Thy free spirit.

O GOD of hope, fill me with all joy and peace in believing, that in this world of mystery, I be not cast down nor dismayed, but may abound in hope in the power of the Holy Spirit; and grant that, laying hold of the hope set before me, it may be to me an anchor of the soul, both sure and steadfast, entering into that which is within the veil; through Jesus Christ my Lord. Amen.

O GOD of hope, I pray for all who are discouraged and depressed, cast down and in despair; for those who are in prison; and for all who have lost the kindly light of reason: let the Sun of Righteousness rise upon them, with healing in His wings. Lord, have mercy upon them and deliver them; through Jesus Christ my Saviour. Amen.

ALMIGHTY God, we beseech Thee, grant unto Thy people grace that they may wait with vigilance for the advent of Thy Son our Lord; that, when He shall arise from Thy right hand to visit the earth in righteousness and Thy people with salvation, He may find us, not sleeping in sin, but diligent in His service and rejoicing in His praises; that so we may enter in with Him unto the marriage of the Lamb; for the merits of the same Jesus Christ our Lord. Amen.

EXTEMPORE PRAYER AND THE LORD'S PRAYER

TWENTY-SIXTH DAY, MORNING   *LOVE*

Hear, O Israel, the Lord our God is one Lord; and thou shalt love the Lord thy God with all thy heart, and with all thy soul, and with all thy mind, and with all thy strength.

Lord, have mercy upon me, and incline my heart to keep this law.

Thou shalt love thy neighbour as thyself.

Lord, have mercy upon me, and incline my heart to keep this law.

A new commandment I give to you, that you love one another, even as I have loved you.

Lord, have mercy upon me, Christ have mercy upon me,

Lord, have mercy upon me, and write all these Thy laws in my heart, I beseech Thee, Amen.

O GOD, who hast taught us to keep all Thy heavenly commandments by loving Thee and our neighbours; grant us the Spirit of peace and grace, that we may be both devoted to Thee with our whole heart, and united to each other with a pure will; through Jesus Christ our Lord. Amen.

SCRIPTURE READING AND MEDITATION

EXTEMPORE PRAYER

FOR THE love of husbands and wives; parents and children; brothers, sisters, and kindred; and especially for these members of my own family which I name before Thee . . .:

I thank Thee, O God.

For all those who love me and help me by word, deed, and example:

I thank Thee, O God.

For all those I love; for neighbours, acquaintances, fellow-workers; for my own personal friends; for all my brethren in Christ:

I thank Thee, O God.

For Thy love manifested in the grace of the Lord Jesus Christ and in the fellowship of the Holy Spirit.
    Thanks be to Thee, O God. Amen.

TWENTY-SIXTH DAY, EVENING   *JOY*

SCRIPTURE READING AND MEDITATION

Thy steadfast love, O Lord, extends to the heavens,
Thy faithfulness to the clouds.
Thy righteousness is like the mountains of God,
Thy judgements are like the great deep;
man and beast Thou savest, O Lord.
How precious is Thy steadfast love, O God!
The children of men take refuge in the shadow of Thy wings.
They feast on the abundance of Thy house.
and Thou givest them drink from the river of Thy delights.
For with Thee is the fountain of life; in Thy light do we see light.
O continue Thy steadfast love to those who know Thee,
and Thy salvation to the upright of heart!

GRANT unto us, O God, the royalty of inward happiness, and the serenity which comes from living close to Thee. Daily renew in us the sense of joy, and let Thy Spirit dwell in our hearts; that we may bear about with us the infection of a good courage, and may meet all life's ills and accidents with gallant and high-hearted happiness, giving Thee thanks always for all things; through Jesus Christ our Lord. Amen.

GRACIOUS FATHER, we humbly beseech Thee for Thy holy catholic Church. Fill it with all truth; and in all truth with all peace. Where it is corrupt purge it; where it is in error, direct it; where it is superstitious, rectify it; where anything is amiss, reform it; where it is right, strengthen and confirm it; where it is in want, furnish it; where it is divided and rent asunder, make up the breaches of it, O Thou Holy One of Israel; for the sake of Jesus Christ our Lord and Saviour. Amen.

EXTEMPORE PRAYER

O Lord Jesus Christ come to me in the morning and shed on the day Thy resurrection light; come to me in the evening and give me Thy peace. May the joy of Thy presence hallow all my days; for Thy name's sake. Amen.

TWENTY-SEVENTH DAY, MORNING   PEACE

Glory be to God on high: and in earth peace, goodwill towards men.

We praise Thee, we bless Thee, we worship Thee, we glorify Thee, we give thanks to Thee for Thy great glory, O Lord God, heavenly King: God the Father almighty.

O Lord, the only-begotten Son, Jesus Christ: O Lord God, Lamb of God, Son of the Father, that takest away the sins of the world, have mercy upon us.

Thou that takest away the sins of the world: have mercy upon us.

Thou that takest away the sins of the world: receive our prayer.

Thou that sittest at the right hand of God the Father, have mercy upon us.

For Thou only art holy: Thou only art the Lord; Thou only, O Christ, with the Holy Spirit, art most high in the glory of God the Father. Amen.

SCRIPTURE READING AND MEDITATION

O God, fill me with Thy Holy Spirit, that I may rejoice in the Lord Jesus always, and have no anxiety about anything, but in everything by prayer and supplication with thanksgiving, let my requests be made known to Thee; and grant that Thy peace, which passes all understanding, may keep my heart and my mind in Christ Jesus. Amen.

O Lord Jesus Christ, who didst say unto Thine apostles, Peace I leave with you, My peace I give unto you; regard not our sins but the faith of Thy Church, and grant unto her that peace and unity which is agreeable to Thy will, who livest and reignest with the Father and the Holy Spirit, God for ever and ever. Amen.

O GOD of peace, grant me Thy grace, that I may live peaceably with all, this day and evermore; for Jesus Christ's sake. Amen.

EXTEMPORE PRAYER AND THE LORD'S PRAYER

TWENTY-SEVENTH DAY, EVENING   PATIENCE

I lift up my eyes to the hills. From whence does my help come?
My help comes from the Lord, who made heaven and earth.
He will not let your foot be moved, He who keeps you will not slumber.
Behold, He who keeps Israel will neither slumber nor sleep.
The Lord is your keeper; the Lord is your shade on your right hand.
The sun shall not smite you by day, nor the moon by night.
The Lord will keep you from all evil; He will keep your life.
The Lord will keep your going out and your coming in from this time forth and for evermore.

O GOD, who art light eternal; I beseech Thee to shed the blessed beams of Thy truth upon my understanding, that by instruction of Thy word I may know Thy will, and be made wise unto salvation; through Jesus Christ my Lord. Amen.

SCRIPTURE READING AND MEDITATION

EXTEMPORE PRAYER

GIVE unto me, O most blessed Lord Jesus, the grace to be patient as Thou wast patient; that I may gently bear with the faults of others, and strive at all times to root out my own; for Thy mercy's sake. Amen.

BLESSED Lord, who Thyself didst undergo the pain and suffering of the cross: uphold, I beseech Thee, with Thy promised gift of strength all those of our brethren who are suffering for their faith in Thee. Grant that in the midst of their persecutions they may hold fast by this faith, and that from their steadfastness Thy Church may grow in grace, and we ourselves increase in perseverance, to the honour of Thy name; who with the Father and the Holy Spirit art ever one God. Amen.

O GOD, since we are surrounded by so great a cloud of witnesses, help us to lay aside every weight, and sin which clings so closely, and to run with patience the race that is set before us, looking to Jesus the Pioneer and Perfecter of our faith. Amen.

TWENTY-EIGHTH DAY, MORNING   *KINDNESS*

Make a joyful noise to the Lord, all the lands!
Serve the Lord with gladness! Come into His presence with singing!
Know that the Lord is God! It is He that made us, and we are His; we are His people, and the sheep of His pasture.
Enter His gates with thanksgiving, and His courts with praise!
Give thanks to Him, bless His name!
For the Lord is good; His steadfast love endures for ever, and His faithfulness to all generations.

SCRIPTURE READING AND MEDITATION

O THOU God of love, who makest Thy sun to rise on the evil and on the good, and sendest rain on the just and on the unjust, and art kind unto the unthankful, grant by Thy Holy Spirit that we may become more and more Thy true children, by receiving into our souls more of Thine own Spirit of ungrudging and unwearying kindness; through Jesus Christ our Lord. Amen.

FOR THY mercies which are new every morning:
For the gift of this new day which lies before me:
For the people I shall meet and for the tasks to be done:
   I thank Thee, O God, through Jesus Christ my Lord. Amen.

HEAR OUR humble prayer, O God, for all animals, especially for those in whose companionship and service we find joy and help. We entreat for them Thy mercy and pity, and for those who deal with them we ask a heart of compassion, gentle hands, and kindly words. Make us all to be true friends of animals, and to share the blessing of the merciful; for the sake of Thy Son, Jesus Christ our Lord. Amen.

EXTEMPORE PRAYER

HEAVENLY FATHER, who hast showed me what is good, and what Thou dost require of me; help me this day and always to do justice, to love kindness, and to walk humbly with Thee my God. Amen.

TWENTY-EIGHTH DAY, EVENING — GOODNESS

SCRIPTURE READING AND MEDITATION

HAVE mercy on me, O God, according to Thy steadfast love; according to Thy abundant mercy blot out my transgressions. Wash me thoroughly from my iniquities, and cleanse me from my sin. For I know my transgressions, and my sin is ever before me. Purge me with hyssop, and I shall be clean: wash me, and I shall be whiter than snow. Create in me a clean heart, O God; and put a new and right spirit within me. Cast me not away from Thy presence; and take not Thy Holy Spirit from me. Amen.

O LORD, from whom all good things do come; grant unto us, Thy humble servants, that by Thy holy inspiration we may think those things that be good; and by Thy merciful guiding may perform the same; through Jesus Christ our Lord. Amen.

HEAVENLY FATHER, I pray for all young people, especially for ... Strengthen them with might by Thy Holy Spirit, that they may ever seek what is true, see what is beautiful, love what is pure, and follow what is right, for the sake of Him who is Truth and Loveliness, Purity and Righteousness, even Jesus Christ our Lord. Amen.

O LORD Jesus Christ, who art the way, the truth, and the life: suffer us not, we pray Thee, to wander from Thee who art the way, nor to distrust Thee who art the truth, nor to rest in any other than Thee who art the life. Teach us what to do, what to believe, and wherein to take our rest; for Thy name's sake. Amen.

EXTEMPORE PRAYER

LORD, now lettest Thou Thy servant depart in peace, according to Thy word; for mine eyes have seen Thy salvation which Thou hast prepared in the presence of all peoples, a light for revelation to the Gentiles, and for glory to Thy people Israel.

Glory be to the Father, and to the Son, and to the Holy Spirit: As it was in the beginning, is now, and ever shall be, world without end. Amen.

TWENTY-NINTH DAY, MORNING   FAITHFULNESS

Blessed be God. Blessed be His holy name.

Blessed be the Lord, the God of Israel, from everlasting to everlasting.

Blessed be God, because He has not rejected my prayer, or removed His steadfast love from me.

Blessed be the Lord, who daily bears us up; God is our salvation.

Blessed be the Lord, the God of Israel, who alone does wondrous things.

Blessed be His glorious name for ever; may His glory fill the whole earth.

Blessed be the name of the Lord from this time forth and for evermore!

From the rising of the sun to its setting, the name of the Lord is to be praised.

ALMIGHTY and most merciful God, the fountain of all goodness, who knowest the thoughts of my heart, I confess that I have sinned against Thee and done evil in Thy sight. Forgive me, O Lord, I beseech Thee, and cleanse me from the stains of all my past offences. Give me grace and power to put away all hurtful things; so that being delivered from the bondage of sin, I may bring forth fruits worthy of repentance. Hear me, O God, I beseech Thee; through Jesus Christ my Lord. Amen.

SPEAK, Lord, for Thy servant heareth. Amen.

SCRIPTURE READING AND MEDITATION

EXTEMPORE PRAYER

LORD JESUS, help me by Thy Spirit to be loyal to my family, friends, and neighbours, and to be reliable and trustworthy as a worker, a citizen, and a member of Thy Church; that in all things I may show fidelity unto Thee, who art Faithful and True. To Thee be glory and dominion for ever. Amen.

GO BEFORE us, O Lord, in all our doings with Thy most gracious favour, and further us with Thy continual help; that in all our works begun, continued, and ended in Thee, we may glorify Thy holy name, and finally by Thy mercy obtain everlasting life; through Jesus Christ our Lord. Amen.

TWENTY-NINTH DAY, EVENING   GENTLENESS

Eternal Light, shine into my heart,
Eternal Goodness, deliver me from evil,
Eternal Power, be my support,
Eternal Wisdom, scatter the darkness of my ignorance,
Eternal Pity, have mercy upon me;
that with all my heart and mind and soul and strength I may seek Thy face and be brought by Thine infinite mercy to Thy holy presence; through Jesus Christ my Lord. Amen.

SCRIPTURE READING AND MEDITATION

O SAVIOUR, meek and lowly of heart, help me to be gentle, courteous, and considerate in speech and action, after Thine own example to all, and for Thy dear sake. Amen.

ETERNAL GOD, our heavenly Father, I pray for our country and all who dwell therein; for our Queen Elizabeth, and all who under her are in positions of authority and responsibility, that they may be guided by Thy pure and peaceable wisdom:
I pray for our soldiers, sailors, and airmen, that they may be sustained in all perils and hardships with courage and endurance; and being guarded by Thy Spirit from all evil, may be strong to do and defend the right:
I pray for the sick, the suffering, and the sorrowful, especially those known and dear to me; that it may please Thee to heal, cheer, and succour them:

I pray for those from whom distance now separates me, that we may be kept in unbroken fellowship in Thee; and for all who have wronged me, that they may be forgiven:

Hear me, I beseech Thee, O Lord. Amen.

EXTEMPORE PRAYER

O GOD, the protector of all that trust in Thee, without whom nothing is strong, nothing is holy: increase and multiply upon us Thy mercy; that, Thou being our ruler and guide, we may so pass through things temporal, that we finally lose not the things eternal; grant this, O heavenly Father, for Jesus Christ's sake our Lord. Amen.

THIRTIETH DAY, MORNING   *SELF-CONTROL*

ALMIGHTY GOD, whose glory the heavens are telling, the earth Thy power, and the sea Thy might, and whose greatness all creatures that think and feel everywhere proclaim: to Thee belong all glory, honour, might, greatness, and splendour, now and for ever, world without end. Amen.

O LORD open Thou my lips and my mouth shall show forth Thy praise: open Thou my mind that I may be enlightened by the truth of Thy word: open Thou my heart, that I may receive the fulness of Thy grace; through Jesus Christ my Saviour. Amen.

SCRIPTURE READING AND MEDITATION

O ETERNAL GOD, who hast made all things subject to man, and man for Thy glory, sanctify our souls and bodies, our thoughts and our intentions, our words and actions, that whatsoever we shall think or speak or do, may be by us designed for the glory of Thy name. Let no pride or self-seeking, no covetousness or revenge, no mean ambitions or low imaginations, desecrate what Thou hast hallowed: but let our body be the servant of our spirit, and both body and spirit servants of Jesus: that doing all things for Thy glory here, we may be partakers of Thy glory hereafter; through Jesus Christ our Lord. Amen.

ALMIGHTY GOD, who seest that we have no power of ourselves to help ourselves: keep us both outwardly in our bodies and inwardly in our souls; that we may be defended from all adversities which may happen to the body, and from all evil thoughts which may assault and hurt the soul; through Jesus Christ our Lord. Amen.

EXTEMPORE PRAYER

LORD Jesus, think through my mind, speak through my lips, work through my hands, and love through my heart, today and always. Amen.

THIRTIETH DAY, EVENING   REVERENCE

HOLY, holy, holy, is the Lord God almighty, who was and is and is to come!

Worthy art Thou, our Lord and God, to receive glory and honour and power, for Thou didst create all things, and by Thy will they existed and were created.

Great and wonderful are Thy deeds, O Lord God the Almighty! Just and true are Thy ways, O King of the ages!

Who shall not fear and glorify Thy name, O Lord? For Thou alone art holy.

All nations shall come and worship Thee, for Thy judgements have been revealed.

Hallelujah! For the Lord our God the Almighty reigns. Let us rejoice and exult and give Him the glory.

Blessing and glory and wisdom and thanksgiving and honour and power and might be to our God for ever and ever. Amen.

HOLY FATHER, let Thy fear come over all Thy creatures, and reverent awe of Thee upon all that Thou hast made, that all Thy creatures may revere Thee and every being bow before Thee, and hallow Thy glorious name, and that they may all become bounded together to do Thy will with all their heart: for Thine is the kingdom, the power, and the glory, for ever and ever. Amen.

SCRIPTURE READING AND MEDITATION

EXTEMPORE PRAYER

O LORD my God, I pray Thee at this evening hour to take my family and friends, and all those who are near and dear to me, into Thy holy keeping. Be pleased to cover their sins with Thy mercy, as Thou dost cover the earth with Thy darkness. Grant them quiet and refreshing sleep this night, and the strength, wisdom and joy of the Holy Spirit all through the coming day. Guard them from all evil, incline them to all virtue and goodness, teach them to know and do Thy will day by day, and bring them at last to Thy eternal kingdom; through Jesus Christ my Lord. Amen.

THIRTY-FIRST DAY, MORNING   *GRATITUDE*

ALMIGHTY GOD, Father of all mercies; we Thine unworthy servants do give Thee most humble and hearty thanks for all Thy goodness and lovingkindness to us and to all men. We bless Thee for our creation, preservation, and all the blessings of this life; but above all, for Thine inestimable love in the redemption of the world by our Lord Jesus Christ, for the means of grace, and for the hope of glory. And we beseech Thee, give us that due sense of all Thy mercies, that our hearts may be unfeignedly thankful, and that we show forth Thy praise, not only with our lips, but in our lives, by giving up ourselves to Thy service, and by walking before Thee in holiness and righteousness all our days; through Jesus Christ our Lord, to whom with Thee and the Holy Spirit be all honour and glory, world without end. Amen.

SCRIPTURE READING AND MEDITATION

O LORD, who hast made us a royal priesthood that we might offer intercession for all men; hear us when we pray:
That it may please Thee to rule and govern Thy holy Church universal in the right way:
That it may please Thee to illumine all ministers, missionaries, evangelists, and teachers with true knowledge and right understanding of Thy word, that both by their preaching and living they may set it forth, and show it accordingly:

That it may please Thee to keep and strengthen in the true worshipping of Thee, in righteousness and holiness of life, Thy servant Elizabeth our Queen:

That it may please Thee to endue our legislators with wisdom and understanding, and to give grace to our judges and magistrates, to execute justice and to maintain truth:

That it may please Thee to give all nations, unity, peace, and concord:

We beseech Thee to hear us, good Lord. Amen.

EXTEMPORE PRAYER AND THE LORD'S PRAYER

THIRTY-FIRST DAY, EVENING   SELF-EXAMINATION

SCRIPTURE READING AND MEDITATION

GOD spake these words and said: I am the Lord Thy God.
Thou shalt have none other gods but Me:
Thou shalt not make to thyself any graven image:
Thou shalt not take the Name of the Lord Thy God in vain:
Remember the Sabbath day to keep it holy:
Honour thy father and thy mother:
Thou shalt do no murder:
Thou shalt not commit adultery:
Thou shalt not steal:
Thou shalt not bear false witness against thy neighbour:
Thou shalt not covet anything that is thy neighbour's:
Merciful God, I acknowledge and confess that I have broken Thy holy law, for there is not one commandment which I have not trangressed in act or in spirit. I have not worshipped and served Thee with all my heart, nor have I loved my neighbour as myself. Lord, have mercy upon me, and write all these Thy laws in my heart, I beseech Thee. Amen.

THANKS be to Thee, my Lord Jesus Christ, for all the benefits Thou hast won for me, for all the pains and insults Thou hast borne for me. O most merciful Redeemer, Friend, and Brother, may I know Thee more clearly, love Thee more dearly, and follow Thee more nearly; for ever and ever. Amen.

EXTEMPORE PRAYER

Remember, O God, what Thou hast wrought in us and not what we deserve: and, as Thou hast called us to Thy service, make us worthy of our calling; through Jesus Christ our Lord. Amen.

> God be in my head, and in my understanding:
> God be in mine eyes, and in my looking:
> God be in my mouth, and in my speaking:
> God be in my heart, and in my thinking:
> God be at mine end, and at my departing. Amen.